HOW TO BE A
GOD-*Wife*

NOT JUST A
"GOOD *Wife*"

April Young

Exulon
ELITE

www.xulonpress.com

Endorsement

"The God-Wife" is a transformational tool tasked with the extraordinary responsibility of not simply impacting, but encouraging "better" to come forth from its readers. This literary weapon arms us with the truth. The ability, authority, and power to retrieve the "better" that we've sought for ourselves and our spouses for so long resides within. This work assists in granting access to our marital destiny through its keys, and challenges our courage against our complacency. If you want more, if you've prayed for better, and if you long to be a "God-Wife"...I humbly propose these instructions: 1) Open your heart 2) Begin on page number one 3) Watch God Move.

God Bless!
#SeekStrengthenShow
Lead Servant- (C4C) Chosen For Completion
Pastor Nate Griffin

This book is dedicated to the jewels in my life
Jailen and Skye

Contents

Foreword

*I*n a day and age where marriage as God ordained it is under attack. The divorce rate both in the church and in secular communities is unconceivable and being single or shacking is becoming more appealing than marriage because of the horrific example that has been demonstrated. A book solidifying that marriage based on Godly principles is not only sustainable but blissful is refreshing. April Young in her book, How to be a God-Wife, Not Just a Good Wife, gives us hope once again.

It was God who decided that man could not or should not live alone. It was God's idea to give man a wo-man (wife) as a companion and not another man, animal or job; and it was God's idea that the wife be a help mate to the man He created. So how does that work? How do two separate individuals, both made in the image and likeness of God become one flesh and manifest the kind of marriage that will have the world saying, "I want what they have." It comes through knowledge…correct knowledge. If we want to experience marriage the way God ordained it, then it is absolutely paramount that we stick to the book…His book. The scripture says to compare yourself with others is not wise (Corinthians 10:12), meaning it's dangerous to allow the world to squeeze us into a mold (Romans 12:2). God defines marriage, not the world and God conveys His idea of a wife, not the world. It is apparent that God has given April Young *intel* that comes straight from heaven. I am so grateful that this book exists. I only wish it was available 21 years ago when my husband and I were ladled with fears and false expectations that were leading us to divorce after less than a year of marriage. We, like most people, had to learn the hard way…with painful scars and some scars don't heal as easily as others. April's understanding of the journey that leads to marital bliss, which ultimately extends from being molded into what that "God-wife", is ladled with oil. The contents of this book, read carefully with a mind of transformation, will not only deliver a solid relationship between man and a woman and God. Yes, husbands are in for a treat once their wives have intimated with this book. Every person who reads this book whether male or female, married or single will benefit from this book. This is wisdom from above that will make you not only build a better person, but build a better you; the one God had on His mind when He placed you on this earth. Yes, marriage between a man and a woman is ordained of God and has great rewards, but it will only happen when you become a God-wife, God husband or more emphatically, a God-child. This book is stellar…straight from the heart of God. Well done April!

Belinda G. Moss, PhD
Teacher, Author, & Personal Mastery Consultant

Acknowledgements

There are many people that have been in my life that in one form or another that have been instrumental in my life. Family at the end of the day are there for you no matter what. However, there are those outside of the family that are just as important. The combination of both helped to make me who I am today. I consider myself beyond blessed.

I want to give my special gratitude to my Redeemer, the Lover of my soul, my Savior, Christ Jesus. It is in Him that I live, move, and have my being. I would like to give a special thank you to my man of God, my best friend and confidant, my husband Micheal. Thank you for your love and encouragement throughout the years. There is not a day that goes by that you do not make me laugh and make me feel like a queen. You truly keep my spirit high. I love you. I want to thank my children, Jare'l and Lauren you have made it so easy to be your mom. I love you and I am extremely proud of you both.

Thank you to Fretta Bass, Minister Francine Douglas, Dora Holloway, Vivian Green-Brown, and Kay Corbi. All of you women have beautiful and altogether lovely spirits. Thank you to the Karen's in my life; Karen Banks, Karen Palmer, and Karen Grissom. Each of you are a blessing in my life. Thank you for being true sister/friends. To my sisters, Brigette and Carla you are always there as a great support system for me. I love you! To my other siblings, Will, Mark, and Mikasha, thank you for loving me the way that you do. Thank you to my mentor Dr. Natalie Francisco, who has spoken into my life many times and has shown me the example of a God-wife. Thank you to Dr. Belinda Moss, your words of wisdom have more than encouraged me. I knew from the moment I met you that there was a connection. I not only consider you a mentor, but a walking power house. You have made an impression on me, as well as other women. You rock. A very heartfelt thank you to Tuwanna Ralph and your mother, Ms. Sycamore. The both of you will always have a special place in my heart.

To an awesome and highly anointed Pastor James T. Elam Jr. and his beautiful wife Lady Penny, you have the heart of God. Thank you so much for your spiritual guidance and leadership. A special thank you to Vicki Yohe, not only are you a gifted and anointed gospel artist and full of the Word, you are a dear friend. I love you! A special gratitude goes out to Charlette Crowell. Thank you so much for the tedious task of editing my manuscript. You are so amazing and I love you.

Lastly, but certainly not least, giving honor where honor is due, my parents, my father, Thomas Harrison, and his wife Minnie. My mother, Dr. Gloria Keene, and her husband, Bill. You all have instilled values into my life that I will forever cherish. You have given me memories that are everlasting. I love you with all my heart.

Introduction

*"Joyfully the radiant bride turned to him, the one
altogether lovely the chief among ten thousand to her
soul, and with unconcealed eagerness to begin her
life of sweet companionship with him, she answered,
make haste, my beloved, and come quickly, like a
gazelle or a young hart and take me to our waiting
home upon the mountains of spices!"*

(Song of Solomon 8:14)

When you say the famous words "I do", what does that really mean? Does it mean that you will do everything you are told to do or expected to do according to your new husband? For centuries many cultures have had their expectations of how a wife is supposed to behave. Who set the standard? Does that standard fit every situation? Or, can this be a successful partnership between husband and wife?

Well, I am about to tell you that there is a better way to live as a happy wife that can lead to a happy life, not just for you but for your husband as well. Being a wife has its perks, however, it has its challenges as well. Now, let's take a look back to that eventful and marvelous day when the excitement is high and you have made up your mind that you are going to live happily ever after with your "Prince Charming" and life is going to be GRAND.

There is just one problem with that...it never happens! Somewhere, someone forgot to attach the warning labels that there will be hard days with bumps in the road and there will not be perfect days every day. You see, when the "honeymoon" is over reality sets in and you are now learning what it is like to live with your "Prince Charming" and he is learning what it is like to live with you as well. Now begins the teachable moment that will forever change the course of your marriage.

You will discover the importance of setting the tone in your home. It is so important that you set the atmosphere for your husband in your home. Marriage is not "fifty-fifty", it is a one hundred percent effort on the husband and wife. Marriage is a partnership that requires work. You God-wife, are instrumental in contributing to the success of your marriage. In this book I discuss demonstrating your Christian walk and understanding the power of unity and walking on one accord. Investing in intimacy is another important factor that I discuss. It is not just for the bedroom. More importantly, our intimate time with the Father is also crucial. He loves when we spend time and love on Him. I will also discuss forgiveness and dealing with your hurt feelings concerning your spouse. In marriage communication is key. Men and women interpret information differently, so I devote a chapter to break down verbal and non-verbal communication. I also speak about the dynamics of a "God-wife" and her value. She puts God first above all else, displays virtue always, and upholds values consistently.

I pray that everything that you read in this book will not only challenge you but compel you to be that "God-wife" God created and fashioned you to be. I can promise you that the road will not be easy, however, it can be one of the most rewarding things that will happen to you. Although I wrote this book with the wife in mind, the single woman will not only benefit, but be prepared and equipped when that special day happens for her. Husbands get ready... you are about to see a change that will bless your socks off! Believe in the blessing and walk in the promises of God for your life together. In this book there are nuggets that will help you to continue to walk by faith and not by sight. A wife is a woman of tremendous influence and power. Her connection and fellowship with the Father is the instrument that makes her marriage flow in beautiful harmony.

One

*She looks well to the ways of her household, and eats not
the bread of idleness Proverbs 31:27*

*The Importance of Setting
the Tone of Your Home*

As women we deal with the daily issues of getting the children ready for school, taking care of the home, and if you work outside of the home you have that responsibility as well. You may ask yourself, "Is there enough of me to go around?"

Guess what? With the proper planning and attitude there is enough of you to go around! Oftentimes, we hear about that Proverbs 31 woman who seemed to be that perfect and intangible person that sounds unreachable. Who was this woman and how do I measure up? Well, she was a woman that had her priorities together. Not only was she a business woman, but she was well respected in the community and revered by her husband. Ultimately, we desire the same respect and love from our husbands.

However, as women, we can't allow the issues of the day affect the way that we treat and respond to our spouse. As I look back on things now I have had a couple of virtuous examples before me growing up. One of which, was my paternal grandmother who lived in North Carolina. I would go with my sisters every summer and spend time on her farm.

My grandmother would rise early at dawn every morning and prepare a hearty breakfast that would stick to the ribs until lunch, go out into the fields and work all day and then come in and prepare a full course meal for the family. She made sure there was order in the house and that her children were well behaved and more importantly, made sure they went to church every Sunday. It did not matter what you did or where you went Saturday night, you were going to church Sunday, no excuses.

I saw such strength in her that she made an impression on me to want to take care of my household. There would be times when I wouldn't see my grandfather for days end and no matter when he came in, she would always ask him if he was hungry and if he said yes she would get up and fix him a plate.

I never once saw them argue or have a disagreement. That doesn't mean that they never had them, it just means that they never did it in front of us. The other example was my Mother. She set the tone for how I would be as a wife and mother. She worked outside of the home, but she always made sure she took care of home. She was a teacher and as trying as that job can be, she never lost focus on the fact that her own children needed her. In addition she made sure we had piano lessons, and encouraged us in girl scouts activities. She taught us the value of reading and how to enjoy a good book, by regular visits to the public library. She spent quality time with us at parks and Bluebird Gap Farm. She instilled in us the love for God through regular church attendance, bible study, and youth program activities. She made clothes for us and made from scratch home cooked meals.

She showed me how a woman is to treat her husband, how to love, honor and cherish him in spite of. Both women were different in many ways but they both shared the same common denominator, they Loved God first and loved family second. They both were selfless in their ways meaning, that they put their needs last.

Today things have changed so much. Women now are single mothers generally surviving off of one income and trying to balance work and family. To my surprise, many women today do not have cooking or meal planning on their agendas. We live in a microwave society where everything has to be quick. I happen to have a husband that is a qualified, skilled chef. However, that does not mean that I do not cook. I have been blessed to be a stay at home wife and my husband, Micheal works outside of the home and attends school full time.

Now, as a virtuous woman, I get up at dawn and prepare his breakfast and his lunch every day. Now mind you, I didn't say I feel like getting up every morning, I make a choice to get up. Why? It is simple. It is not about me but about making sure the needs of my husband are being met. You see, when we choose to say "I do," the mindset of "it's all about me" goes right out the window! Marriage is a commitment and a partnership. It takes compromise and lots of effort to make it work. For so long we have heard the phrase "Marriage is "fifty-fifty." That could not be further from the truth.

Marriage is about spouses giving each other one hundred percent. In order to do that there must be two complete people coming together and be willing parties who commit to a life-long journey of making it work. When God is the center of the marriage union you have the main ingredient that will produce a fruitful outcome.

It is also important to set the tone by praying for and over your family. The enemy is very cunning in his ways. He will use whatever tactic to cause division, confusion and discord in your home. It maybe something as simple as causing your children to rebel and become unruly.

Satan does not discriminate when it comes to causing discord. You have to be ready as the woman God called you to be. Remember, we have that intuitive gift, use it! The enemy is the author of confusion… God is not. Satan is the accuser of the brethren. Your husband is the defender and protector and you as his wife, are his help meet, so if he is the President then surely you know your place as the Vice President. What happens if the President of the United States is unable to handle a certain task? The Vice president has to step up to the plate and carry out the task.

We as women have to step up in warrior mode and defend and protect using what God has equipped us with… prayer and the Word. That is a double team of mass destruction against the enemy. This is war and with that kind of power, we win every time.

Prayer
Father, give me the discernment to recognize the enemy and to stand my ground concerning any attack against my marriage. As a united front, we win in Jesus' name, Amen.

Two

Do not be unequally yoked with unbelievers: for what fellowship have righteousness and unrighteousness? Or what communion has light with darkness? (2 Corinthians 6: 14) MEV

Equally Yoked

When choosing a mate we are often taught to make sure the person is equally yoked with our beliefs. In many cases that does not always hold true. When Paul spoke to the Corinthian church he was referring to the practice of paganism with non-believers and he encouraged them to not fellowship with those, unbelievers, *apistos "without Christian faith", those considered to be faithless.* It is assumed that *"unequally yoked"* is a connotation for marriage. However, it can be used to apply to marriage when having a mate. There are couples who come together already in Christ and have a committed relationship in the Word. However, there are times when one spouse may come to know the Lord but the other hasn't. Does that mean that is a cause for divorce? Absolutely not.

The actions of how you demonstrate your Christian walk will win that spouse to Christ giving them both the opportunity to experience the life and love of Christ together. Being equally yoked matters on so many levels. It makes things easier when you are working on a common goal and are able to face challenges together as a united front. The best example of an equally yoked couple would be the very first couple mentioned in the Bible, Adam and Eve.

And the Lord God said. "It is not good that man should be alone; I will make him a helper comparable to him." (Genesis 2:18). Comparable means to be likened to another, similar, equivalent, close, having features in common with something else. And Jehovah God caused a deep sleep to fall upon the man, and he slept; and He took one of his ribs, and closed up the flesh instead thereof: and the rib which Jehovah God had taken from the man, made he a woman, and brought her unto the man. And the man said, *"This is now bone of my bones, and flesh of my flesh: she shall be called Woman, because she was taken out of Man." Therefore shall a man leave his father and his mother, and shall cleave unto his wife: and they shall be one flesh (Genesis 2:19-24).*

Adam understood that Eve was a part of him formed by God in His image. They both communed with God and they were comparable. It was evident that they were equal. They would also be the first examples of best friends. Just imagine that there was no one else on the earth except for the animals that Adam named himself. Can you imagine the conversations they would have and the things they explored together in the Garden of Eden? To make things more glorious, they walked with God! A life with no worries or concerns until the enemy came to cause discord. Eve recognized after the fact that she was deceived by the enemy and as with any union there will be days when your faith and love for one another will be tested.

Just imagine a life where God picks the perfect mate, chose the perfect home and provided everything you could possibly need to live. When God's hand is upon it, it is blessed. Then all of a sudden, the enemy comes in and causes a divide, not only with you and your husband, but with you and your Heavenly Father. It goes to show you how cunning the enemy was during Adam and Eve's time. It is no different from his cunning ways of today. It is important to understand the power of unity and walking in one accord. What would have been the turn of events if Eve had said no to the serpent and was obedient to what God had asked of her and Adam? God is an all knowing God and He knew that the sin of disobedience would take place and He knew the consequences of such actions.

The husband is Satan's worst nightmare because the husband is the head and Satan hates authority. Why do you think he sought out Eve and not Adam? The best way to get to the head is to get what is closest to him, his help-meet. Satan knew he didn't have a chance if he approached Adam. He knew that Eve would influence Adam and that Adam would take the bait that the enemy had set through Eve. Nevertheless, God held Adam accountable because he was not in his rightful place as the head. A clear example of how obedience is better than sacrifice because Adam and Eve had to sacrifice their freedom and their perfect home for a life of hard work, pain, struggle, and ultimately death.

Prayer

Father, In Your Word it states that a man that finds a wife finds a good thing and obtains favor from You. As Your daughter, I know You have Your very best for me in a mate. Thank You that he is filled with Your spirit and he is the man You designed and created specifically for me and I am designed and created specifically for him. Thank You that my husband and I are obedient to Your will and we recognize the enemy and we stand together as one.
In Jesus' name, Amen.

Three

Investing in Intimacy

(Invest- to provide or endow someone or something with; a particular quality or attribute)

(Intimacy-a close, familiar, and usually affectionate or loving personal relationship with another person or group)

Just as we expect intimacy with our spouse God expects intimacy with us. Imagine how intense our love becomes when we become intensely in love with God. The love and closeness is immeasurable. There is no comparison to any other love we will experience.

When going to the Father with whatever issue or concern, we expect results. However, when we go to Him to commune, fellowship, and love on Him out of gratefulness what a testament! He delights in us as we delight in Him (Psalm 37:4). *"Take delight in the Lord and He will give you your heart's desire" (Psalm 37: 4 NLT Study Bible).* When we invest that time He makes our time with one another effortless. Making love and being intimate will not become a chore, but immense joy.

Recently my husband and I were invited to attend a Covenant Keeper's marriage ministry meeting by a Pastor friend of ours, Pastor Nathaniel Griffin and his wife Lady Ebony. First, let me tell you that more ministries concerning marriages need to exist. Marriages are far too important not to invest in quality time with your spouse. Just imagine when a couple is fully committed to their marriage and then you have couples coming together on one accord, in fellowship, on a corporate level. That is a lot of power in one place! Now, that is what I call the definition of power couples.

The event usually takes place once a month on a Friday night. Dinner is served followed by an activity or assignment for the couples. One particular night the assignment was for the couples to anoint their spouse and pray for their eyes, hands, feet, mouth, ears, and the mind of their spouse. All of this was done during candlelight. Not only was this very significant, but very profound. Let's just explore this for a moment. As wives, we have the awesome responsibility of praying for our husbands. However, have we taken the time to pray for his eyes? That when he looks, he will see through Christ's eyes and have eyes only for you.

Or that when we pray for his feet that he will walk uprightly before the Lord and that wherever he treads his feet, he will have favor and possess the land. Or when we pray for his hands that his hands are anointed and that whatever he puts his hands to will prosper. When we pray for his mind, he will have the mind of Christ and be able to make wise and concise decisions concerning your present and future together.

Remember, we shall have what we say. Words are very powerful, so why not speak them over your husband? If there is an issue with your husband and you want to see a change, do not nag or complain about it. Confess it and believe God. On another Covenant Keeper's fellowship there was an assignment given where the couples were to write a love letter to one another. The couples were not allowed to share the contents of the letter at that time, but instructed to mail it to their spouse

In the process of waiting for the letter the couples were to write something on sticky notes that would let your spouse know how you feel. That could mean putting the sticky on his steering wheel, his computer, his lunch box etc. This went on for a week. The excitement of receiving a love letter in the mail from your spouse brought about a spark that may have been dormant for months or even years.

Think about it, how often do we think of writing a letter and actually mailing it to our spouse? With the everyday issues of life, working, school, and church it is safe to say, hardly ever, if at all. Keeping the spark is very important. You want to make sure that the "love connection" is still alive. Tammy and Todd Barker are a fun couple, full of creative ideas and they are responsible for facilitating Covenant Keeper's Fellowships. They have done a wonderful job with creative assignments by thinking outside of the box ideas for the couples under the leadership of Pastor Nathaniel Griffin.

Just as words are powerful so can actions be. We can choose to have the right attitude toward our spouse or we can choose to have an "attitude". If choosing the latter, somehow it seems fitting to withhold intimacy as a punishment, if you will, and make the other person suffer while you gloat and feel a sense of power or control. Not only is that contrary to the Word of God and what God says, but it is another form of rebellion.

The Word of God states, the husband should not deprive the wife of sexual intimacy, which is her right as a married woman. Nor should the wife deprive her husband. The wife gives authority over her body to her husband, and the husband also gives authority over his body over to his wife. So do not deprive each other of sexual relations. With the exception that they be in agreement of both husband and wife to refrain from sexual intimacy for a limited time to give themselves completely to prayer.

That they may come together again so that the enemy will not be able to tempt them because of their lack of self-control. As always, the enemy comes to steal kill and destroy. What a better way than to cause a divide in intimacy leaving the door open for infidelity for either spouse to be tempted. Remember, the husband and wife are a united front. As a wife, the responsibility is great. It should never be seen as a chore or become so complacent that you live in a miserable state.

Intimacy is not just for the bedroom. It should be displayed throughout the day. Think of it this way, when you are watching a movie or reading a novel they both are building on something and then there is the climax. The climax does not just automatically happen, it is a process. Intimacy needs to be built upon. For example, when your husband leaves for the day, whisper something sweet in his hear to let him know that he is loved. Plant a kiss on his lips and say there is more to come. Now, his mind is already thinking. Then throughout the day send him a text or email that will keep him motivated and ready to come home. I am excited when the clock nears three o clock in the afternoon. Micheal leaves work at that time every day. I greet him every day at the door. I want him to know that I am glad that he is home. There is something that says to your husband, he feels the love and warmth of his home because you, God-wife, make him feel that way.

We as women tend to be emotional and we love the affection and attention from our mate. Believe it or not, most men like affection and physical touch. There is something that happens, a connection that gets them excited and aroused knowing that you long for them. Listen, we have to make sure and cover all bases. Remember, there is always another woman that is willing to show your husband affection and attention whether he wants it or not. Believe me, the fact that he wears a wedding band is not going to stop them from trying. Some women actually like the comfort of knowing that the man is married. We know that it is not right, yet it is a reality that happens every day.

One particular Sunday after church service was over my husband Micheal was standing on the back wall in the sanctuary and I was on the other side of the sanctuary. I looked his way until our eyes met. I gave him a look that made him feel as though we were the only people in the room. I then proceeded to walk toward him, never breaking eye contact. I stood in front of him and said "Excuse me, I do not see your wife, so does that mean I can get your number?" He laughed, and he actually gave me a kiss right there. I said all that, to say this, sometimes you have to be the other chic, the "girlfriend" if you will, just to keep things fresh and interesting. I will be the first to tell you that it takes work and it is not always easy, but taking the extra effort will always outweigh the consequences of never trying.

There will be days when you literally want to strangle your husband and other days you may want to love on him just because. I will be the first to tell you I love my husband Micheal, he is a wonderful man. However, I have days where I find a moment to read or write and as soon as I start I hear the melodious words "Honey, can you come here for a second?" Or "Babe can you do me a quick favor?" That is the moment where my brain will say it never fails, he must time it when I try and steal away a few moments in a book or to catch up on some writing.

Now, I know that may seem trivial to you but everyone has a vice or a pet peeve, if you will. Case and point, I have to make a decision right then that I will keep my attitude in check and see what my husband needs. Never mind the fact that when he is watching a football or basketball game I choose not to interrupt him. That time is precious to him, so unless I am watching the game with him, I let him have his time. That does not mean that I am neglecting what I want to do, it just means it is not always about me.

Being a wife means there are many "self-less" moments and we have to be ADAPTABLE to our mate. Later in the book I will get into the dynamics of a God-wife. There will be times when it is important to spend that time together doing activities such as gardening, taking walks, going out on date nights to dinner or the movies. However, time away from one another is important as well. That doesn't mean long or extended time away. Now, if your spouse is in the Armed Forces that is totally different because they are required to have duty away from the home for extended periods of time. I remember when my husband did his last tour in Iraq and I cried like a baby because he was going to be away from me for seven months.

The thought of him being in danger was enough, but seven months? How dare the military do this to me! Let me tell you, I was definitely in "self". Standing in the airport, Micheal looked at me and said "It will be as if I never left, you will see me and talk to me every day."

That got my attention. I looked up at him and said what are you talking about? He went on to tell me that everything was going to be alright just wait and see. Needless to say, a week later there was a laptop delivered to the house so that we would be able to Skype practically every day. I said all that to say, there are creative ways to connect with your spouse. Even if it looks like it is impossible.

It is vital to keep the flame forever burning. If you are that stay at home wife, your husband wants to come home to a wife that greets him with a smile, not a complaint. He wants to come home to dinner sometimes. You may not be the best cook, but as Pastor James T. Elam Jr. says "Anyone can read a recipe."

Your husband will be appreciative of the attempt to pre-pare a meal for him. He may even like the fact that when he comes home you greet him in a new sexy outfit or nighty that will make him forget that rough day he had at work. This will make him want to hurry home simply because he has no idea what surprise may be waiting for him.

I have heard stories of men who dread the very fact of going home. They may sit in the drive way for thirty min-utes before actually going into the house for fear of some sort of confrontation. The thrill or zest has left the marriage and all hope is seemingly lost.

Although it may look bleak, all is not lost when we as wives stand in our rightful place, seeking God's face, praying for our husbands daily, working the Word, and giving our husband the support and encouragement that he needs. Trust me ladies, when your husband has everything he needs in you; you as a God-wife will lack no good thing.

Prayer

Lord thank you that my husband and I have taken the time to not only invest intimate time with You, but investing time with one another. Keep our minds with creative ideas and a fire that ignites a flame that will never burn out.
In Jesus' name, Amen.

Four

Be gentle and forbearing with one another and, if one has a difference (a grievance or complaint) against one another, readily pardoning each other; even as the Lord has [freely] forgiven you, so must you also [forgive]. (Colossians 3:13 AMP)

Forgiveness First

Forgiveness is not as complex as some would make it. Forgiveness is usually for you, not the other person. In order to move on in our lives in the things that God has for us, we need to forgive first. You have to first know how to forgive yourself for any indiscretions and more importantly, forgive those who may have transgressed against you.

Especially when there is a soul-tie involved. This is a very sensitive issue with the offended spouse. They may not understand that a soul-tie is a stronghold and it needs to be dealt with firmly. Meaning, the enemy needs to be put on notice that should you decide to work on your marriage in spite of the transgression, he has no place in your home and he no longer has control over the spouse that has committed the offense. Prayer and confession is critical in this process.

Remember, infidelity is not just physical, it is also emotional. There are couples that have experienced emotional affairs that have not been physical. Emotional affairs are just as damaging as an actual physical affair because you are mentally connected to that person and they begin to take up a lot of your thought process. The offender becomes emotionally connected and their thoughts are affected because they begin to think about the person that is outside of their marriage.

These feelings will in turn cause the offender to respond indifferently toward their spouse and become obsessive toward the third party. Your morals and character can change because of the soul-tie connection. This is another controlling tactic of Satan. The enemy uses the other woman or man to cause division with you and your mate and his purpose is to destroy the marriage. The soul-tie can be broken when dealt with head on with forgiveness from the offended spouse. As a God-wife, our responsibility is to protect that which God has given us and the anointing that is on our husband and marriage.

Ladies, it is imperative that we recognize the anointing that is on our husband, as well as, recognize the tactics of the enemy. I remember years ago, I had a conversation with Micheal and I remember sharing with him that I recognize the calling that he has on his life and it was confirmed through our former Pastor and his Pastor back home in Mississippi. I distinctly remember saying that the anointing comes with a price and it has to be protected at all cost. There will be women who will be attracted to you because of the anointing. Satan has a way of causing confusion and discord and he doesn't mind sending a distraction by way or in the form of a woman. Believe me, she will have the looks and the words to say just to try and persuade you. The Bible states "Why should you, my son, be infatuated with a loose woman, embrace the bosom of an outsider, and go astray?" Proverbs 5:20 (AMP). We, as wives, recognize when another woman has impure motives and making moves on our husband! However, men are not so quick to clearly see the wiles of the enemy when he is about to set up a trap to get him off course.

No matter what the enemy tries to do, stand firm on the Word of God and use the weapon of prayer like never before!

There is no need to walk around bitter or angry for an offense someone may have done against you. Some marriages may experience infidelity at one time or another. When this happens there is a lot of hurt and the trust level may have gone from one hundred to zero fast. Look at the spirit of the person, and not the person themselves. In such cases it is vital that the offense is forgiven. Be mindful, this will not happen overnight it is a process.

It is okay to reveal your true feelings and not keep them bottled up inside of you. If you hurt then say that you are hurt. There is a freedom in that. However, when you keep it to yourself there is a great danger in that because that is a portal or entry way for the devil to work not only on your heart but your mind.

Satan will take advantage of that situation causing you to harbor anger and resentment. He is no respecter of person when it comes to causing discord with you and your husband. When you and your husband are on one accord and walking in the things of the Lord, you two become a double threat and any way he can get in to destroy what God has put together he seizes the moment. That is why it is key to walk together in unity even if there is a moment that we can agree to disagree, yet still be unified. Trust God no matter what it looks like. God's desire is to always give us His very best. Fear comes about when we doubt or lose sight of the mighty hand of God. It gets distorted by the sly influence of the enemy. Remember, the enemy does well to try and make whatever we are going through appear "big". However, we serve a BIG God that trumps over every issue that leads to TRIUMPH. Holy Spirit is a guide and a teacher. He is able to show us what it is we need to do that which is fail-proof.

There has to be a decision of whether or not to stay together or to end the marriage. A dear friend of mine went through an ordeal where she discovered that her husband was having an affair with one of her friends. She was devastated to say the least. She initially wanted to work things out with her husband and even sought counseling. However, it was made clear to her that her husband had no intentions to stop seeing the other woman.

This ultimately led to their divorce. There has to be a commitment from both parties to want to work things out. Forgiveness plays an important part when making a decision to stay together or divorce. Until forgiveness is evident in the relationship, it is hard to move on.

So many times I have heard the phrase "I can forgive you, but I will never forget what you did." Once again words are so powerful because when you clearly state that you have forgiven someone, there should never be a "but" behind it. When we have committed an offense before God, He does not hold it against us. God is forgiving and our sins are put into the sea of forgetfulness. It is important not to release negativity in your relationship. Exhibit self-control at all times. In forgiveness, God looks at the heart. Jesus was great at letting go of the hurt that others inflicted on

Him. Pray for your offenders and release it to the Father and move on. Jesus did.

We have been given the example in Christ as He is forgiving and filled with compassion. Jesus never turned His back on anyone, even unto His death when He said "Father forgive them for they know not what they do" (Luke 23:34a). With the harsh treatment that our Savior received, He still exhibited forgiveness. We know that Jesus knew that Judas was going to betray Him. He also knew that the plan of the Father had to be fulfilled. We may not understand all that God has planned for us, we just have to trust that He knows what He is doing. To everything there is a plan and purpose for each of us here on the earth.

Who are we not to follow His example? We get offended at words that are spoken to us and maybe quick to get upset and unforgiving. Just imagine the beating and taunting that Jesus received and yet, He was forgiving. That is something to think about. It is so sad that we become angry and upset with a family loved one or friend and we hold on to the offense and go months, sometimes years without speaking to them.

Life is too short and tomorrow is not promised to any of us. Whenever we are given the opportunity to make things right we should move on the chance to do so. We are ultimately held accountable for what we do. Walking uprightly before God should take priority even if we don't get it right every time. Just like the woman who was caught in adultery, Jesus responded to the accusing men by saying to them "He who is without sin among you, let him throw a stone at her first" (John 8:7b). The men threw the stones down and walked away. We all have sinned and fallen short of His glory (Romans 3:23).

Having un-forgiveness and bitterness can lead to sickness in our bodies, frustration and a hardened heart. When you concentrate on establishing a right relationship with God and your spouse He is glorified. Grace has been given to us to endure whatever comes our way concerning the highs and lows of marriage. It is not based on conditions. For example, I will still love you if you stay a size two or I will love you as long as you cook and clean for me.

God is a God of unconditional love not a God that loves us based on conditions. There are three types of love in the Greek. The first one is called Eros *(when there is a physical attraction)*. Second, *Philos, (a friendship, brotherly kind of love). Third, Agape (an unconditional love, God-like love)* When you first meet your spouse I am sure there was eros, and then philos evident. However, when it comes time to commit to marriage all three types should be present, but agape love should out- weigh them all.

Prayer

Father, thank you that I am able to forgive just as You have forgiven me. We all have sinned and fallen short of Your glory. I walk in agape love towards my husband every day. My heart is not hardened toward him and that I walk as an example in Your presence that You may be glorified.

In Jesus' name Amen

Five

"Wives, be submissive to your own husbands as unto the Lord. For the husband is head of the wife, just as Christ is head and Savior of the church, which is His body. But as the church submits to Christ, so also let the wives be to their own husbands in everything" (Ephesians 5:22-24 MEV).

The Other "S" Word

efore writing this chapter I asked family and friends if they knew what the "s" word was. They all assumed it was for the word *sex*. I distinctly knew that was going to be the response when I asked the question. I know this chapter will be the highlight of this book, simply because it will raise eyebrows.

Submission, I believe, is one of the most misunderstood words ever spoken. When you hear this word, some automatically think that it means demeaning or a sign of weakness. However, when you think about it we are all under some type of authority. Submit means the condition of being submissive, humble or compliant. It also means yield to authority or be accountable to another; God, society, or fellow believers.

Let us look at the One who showed the greatest example of submission, Christ. Throughout the Bible Jesus showed that He Himself was under the authority of God, the Father. It is the will of God that we submit to authority. It is in the Word. Remember, we submit to God first. The God-head then to our husband, the head of our home.

In doing so, there is an order to all things and that is being obedient to God first and foremost. In Philippians 2:7-8, Jesus under the authority and obedience to God, stripped Himself taking upon Himself the form of a servant and was made in the likeness of men. Being found in the form of a man, He humbled Himself and became obedient to death even on the cross. As wives, out of humbleness, submit to the authority of your house and receive grace from our Father in heaven, where there is a benefit. Men are not exempt from submission, they too are under authority so no means is this one-sided.

"When you discover how much God really loves you, you then understand magnitude of how to love."

A few years ago one night in particular, I had already retired for the evening and my husband came into our bedroom and wanted me to get him a glass of water. Now, mind you, I had already found my comfortable spot on my pillow. I really did not want to get out of my bed to get him a glass of water, especially when he could have taken his very capable self and gotten that glass of water before he got into the bed. Nevertheless, I got up and went to the kitchen and proceeded to get the glass of water.

Well, let me tell you, obedience is much better than sacrifice. I looked on the counter and there was a card with my name on it and two gift boxes. I was really surprised. The card was very sweet and in each of the gift boxes was a beautiful watch. Just imagine if I had the wrong attitude and said "I am tired and you can get your own water."

That was a test I could have failed miserably if I had gone off of how I felt and out of rebellion refused to get his water. My husband did not really want or need the water. His aim was to be a blessing to me. That is how we are with God. He may give us an instruction that may or may not make sense to us at the time. We then choose to not submit or walk in obedience therefore, missing out on the blessing He has for us.

Just suppose for a moment that your husband wants you to rub his back or his feet and you take on the attitude and say that is beneath me... that is not in my "wifely" job description! Remember, Jesus was a servant and under the authority of the Father. He humbled Himself and washed the feet of His disciples who felt like they, themselves, were not worthy. So I ask you, who are we that we as wives will not be humble and honor a simple request? Once again, submission is not about us and marriage is never a one way street.

You are anointed specifically for your husband. God has made you adaptable and suitable for him. You walk as a united front. How can two walk together except they be agreed? When you become a servant unto God, you become more than capable of serving your husband as unto the Lord.

We do not compete with our husbands, we were made to compliment him as his help-meet. In all things, we must trust, obey, and believe God. Walking in submission covers every area your life because we are covered under the authority of God. As wives, we should always be an example of virtue to our husbands and others.

That by no means is demeaning, nor should it be beneath you. Once again, when we do things as unto the Lord it is not about us and how we feel. We are not just submissive to our husbands, but how many times has your boss or a friend asked something of you and you were more than happy to accommodate them? We do not go home to them, but to our husband, yet we are eager to please their request.

1 Peter 2:13 says, *"Submit yourself to every ordinance or law of man"*. When that police officer is following you in your car with his/her lights flashing, do you stop under his/her authority or do you speed up and keep going? I trust that you quickly analyze the situation and stop the car.

We know that if the car does not come to a complete stop that there will be a consequence. It is the will of God that we submit to authority. It is in the Word. For every action under authority that we do not complete there will always be some sort of consequence.

Remember, we submit to God first, the God-head then to our husband, the head of our home. I know that some of you may say "What if my husband is not saved and does not have a relationship with Christ, why should I submit?" It is simple, even on his worst day, love him to Christ. Your husband will be moved by your example, as well as, your actions. You want that man to lead your family in the Lord as the priest and man of God in your home. I remember a friend of mine's husband loved to say he was the head of his house and his wife quickly responded "Yes dear, but the head can't move without the support of the neck!" I got a revelation in that moment. A family is as strong as the leadership of the husband and father, and the husband is as strong as the God-wife, that supports him at his side. He carries the weight of his family on his shoulders and his responsibility is great. Therefore, with a God-wife at his side, they are unstoppable and they become powerful against the wiles of the enemy.

We can endure the consequences of disobedience or get it right the first time and see the fruits of walking in obedience as unto the Lord. Walking in submission to one another means walking victorious!

Prayer

Heavenly Father, under Your authority, I thank You that I walk in submission to You, first and foremost. Submitting to You, as well as, to my husband will be effortless. As a God-wife, I clothe myself in humility as I walk in total submission to my husband and his vision for our family. I walk in agreement according to Your Word and I am an example before others. I understand that being submitted to my husband means that I am obedient to Your will, therefore enabling me to receive the blessings of a God-wife, as I trust and depend totally on Holy Spirit for discernment on how to be the wife You have called me to be.
In Jesus' name, Amen.

Six

"A gentle answer turns away wrath, but a harsh word stirs up anger" (Proverbs 15:1).

Communication: The Key that Opens the Door

{Communicate-To make known, impart}

{Communication-The exchange of thoughts, messages, or information} (American Heritage Dictionary}

Men and women can interpret information differently. When we were in school we were taught listening skills, therefore it is learned behavior. We are not born to automatically know listening skills. Your attitude and posture are important key factors in communication. Body language is very important and part of non-verbal communication. Listening, however, is the biggest piece of the puzzle. Eye contact, body and facial expressions, gestures, and the pitch of your tone are key factors as well.

Our communication skills can be a direct reflection of what we learned growing up. For instance, you may have grown up with parents that communicated by yelling and screaming at the top of their lungs. Or you may have grown up in a household where feelings were not expressed at all. Nonetheless, we emulate what we see in the home.

Saying the words "I love you" was common and affection evident in some families. However, there are adults today who never heard those words growing up. Therefore, as adults, are unable to say or express love.

I have a few friends and family members who grew up in an era where their father did not express themselves in that way. It seemingly took away from being a man or showed a sign of weakness. Sadly, this hampered young men from showing affection or love to their wife and children. Communication does not have to be eloquent to be understood. It is best to be honest and put everything on the table. My husband and I do not always agree, yet we make it a point to talk things out. We make sure that we do not go to bed angry, no matter what. This may sound a little crazy, but Micheal and I will have a disagreement and five minutes later it will be as if the disagreement never happened. However, you and your husband may need a little more time. Each situation is different.

There may be times when you want to express how you feel without any feedback from your spouse, you just want a listening ear. Sometimes as women the nurturing factor kicks in and we want to offer a solution and your husband only wants to vent. However, there is a way where you can make a suggestion to your husband and have him walk away as if it were his idea! Remember, you are a woman of influence. Delilah had no problem influencing Samson to tell his secret to his strength and she wasn't his wife. So just imagine the power and influence you have!

My husband, Micheal, is very passionate about what he feels. It took me a couple of years after we were married to understand that. So I would take offense and get upset causing a huge gap with our communication. There is a way to communicate with your husband without it sounding like a complaint or that you are nagging him. Holy Spirit is a Revealer and when I am trying to understand Micheal, Holy Spirit will show me how to respond and not react. He also lets me know when my husband is hurt by something he may have said to me. I can also see when Holy Spirit is convicting him concerning me. Holy Spirit will show you your husband's heart so that in turn your heart may be softened toward your husband. When a spouse makes a comment that isn't necessarily a positive comment, it does not mean that it gives us a license to fire back with words that cut and hurt our spouse.

It is our responsibility to recognize that attitude that we have concerning our husband. Allow God's Word to be the determining factor of how we speak to one another. It is important to be able to meet one another half way and sometimes we as wives have to go all the way. We have to also be mindful that sometimes we take on the thought, I want out, I can't deal with my husband. We have already emotionally separated or divorced him. This leaves very little room to communicate effectively. We have shut down to any reasoning and resolving any type of conflict. It is necessary to come together in agreement whether or not your marriage is worth saving. If you know that God has predestined you to be together, then working on it in unity is worth the effort. The enemy has no power or control over your marriage. I have to walk with a spirit of humility simply because I know that it is easy to lash out and try and get my point across. Proverbs 15:1-2 says, "A soft answer turns away wrath: but grievous words stir up anger. The tongue of the wise uses knowledge aright: but the mouth of fools pours out foolishness". We have to overcome evil with good keeping our mouth and soul from trouble.

Your husband needs to feel like he is understood, appreciated, and loved. As his wife you want to feel like you are important, respected, loved, and that how you feel matters. Your husband also needs your encouragement. He needs to know that he is the king of his castle and that you trust him.

As your husband, he needs to understand that you are the queen and that you have order concerning the home and that a happy wife means a happy life.

Paying attention and using eye contact when speaking is very important to me, because I want to know that you are being truthful and what your facial expression is saying. What is your facial expression saying when your husband is speaking? Are you showing compassion or are you rolling your eyes, or being unresponsive? There should not be any distractions, such as the television, other people walking in or out of the room, or texting. It is not a good time to have a conversation with your husband while he is playing Call of Duty.

You may be aggressive and your husband may be passive. In such case, it is always important to consider the other spouse feelings. However, demonstrating assertiveness you can make your point clear without being disrespectful. Your husband wants to know that above all else, YOU RESPECT HIM. A woman doesn't tear down her husband but builds him up. Be mindful that putting your husband down doesn't help the situation should your conversation become at the disagreeable state.

There are some cases where this may be difficult for some wives that try and take over or wear the pants because prior to marriage they were very independent. This makes it hard because you have to share responsibility with another human being. It is ok to allow your husband to take lead as the head of his home. As the wife, it should be seen as a blessing and not a hindrance.

Because my husband and I are very passionate of what we feel, I was constantly saying to him it is not what you say, it is how you say it. Because men and women receive things differently, perception is everything. You can say the same thing without hurting the other. Let's just imagine you were in conversation with Jesus. We know that what-ever He needs to converse with us about we would be on our best behavior and speak to Him with the utmost respect and admiration. If we along with our husband are one with Christ, why wouldn't we show one another the same respect? Jesus was the perfect example of love, patience and compassion. *Proverbs 25:24 "*

"It is better to live alone in the corner of an attic than with a quarrelsome wife in a lovely home". Proverbs 27:15 says, a quarrelsome wife is annoying as a constant dripping on a rainy day. Stopping her complaints is like trying to hold something with greased hands.

In appropriate times, silence is golden. Notice, I did not say the "silent treatment". When I am having a rough day, I like to take a few moments to myself by reading, medi-tating, and believe it or not, cooking. So while I am doing these things I want to be able to relax and settle my mind. The last thing I want to do is get into a heavy or heated discussion. Because I am in tune with my husband, I know when he comes home from a rough day therefore, I am mindful not to bombard him with the matters of the day. I greet him and give him his space and allow him to relax and get comfortable before getting into how my day went.

Once again, body language is everything when determining a good time to converse. There are times when I may not be feeling well, or I may have a headache and I have not verbally communicated it to my husband. Yet, he knows me well enough to know when I am not feeling my best. So many times we can be so excited about what we are dealing with in the course of the day that we neglect the feelings of our spouse.

It is ok to communicate what we desire and want in our spouse, however there is a way to do everything. When there is something that may be bothering you about your spouse, giving them the silent treatment is not the answer. The only thing that you have resorted to is answering with one word answers when asked a question by your husband. It is just the opening that the enemy needs to get in and cause you and your husband to be divided.

I have been guilty of saying when you see me get quiet then that is when you should be concerned. Now, that statement doesn't make me the bigger person. It actually makes me look weak, simply because a strong woman doesn't have an issue with discussing what is wrong. I understand that when we are young and still learning how to be a wife, it is easy to fall into mind and game playing. However, when you are mature and know who you are, game playing is not part of the plan. As the great Maya Angelou once said, "When you know better you do better." There comes a time in our lives when we are in right relationship with Christ, you then have the door open for Holy Spirit to teach you how to respond positively to your husband, instead of reacting negatively.

The God-wife knows and understands that her example becomes effortless when she is led by Hoy Spirit to uphold what is right in the eyesight of the Lord. God's grace is more than sufficient when we are unsure on how to respond to our spouse. I remember Micheal and I had a disagreement about something early in our marriage and I decided that I was going to give him the "silent" treatment. I mean I was going to show him that I was tough and I could go on with my everyday ritual without having to communicate with him. Just so you know, I am married to an "unofficial" comedian who has excellent delivery. He happened to say something that was so hilarious that as hard as I tried, I could not help but laugh... breaking whatever animosity I had with him.

You see, Micheal understands that I can't stay mad at him and that whatever the issue, it is never that serious where we can't confront it. That doesn't mean that he takes me for granted or that he takes lightly my feelings. That just allowed him to break the ice, if you will, so that we can talk out the issue. Every situation is different and your husband may have dry humor and getting you to laugh at a crucial moment may not work for you. For you, your husband may have to get you flowers or a simple apology is needed. Whatever it takes to get you and your husband back on track, it is vital that effective communication is always the key that opens that door to marriage success.

Prayer

Father, thank you that I am able to respond positively to my husband. I am that God-wife that not only communicates with my husband but I recognize my responsibility as a help-meet and that when I speak to him, I have a listening ear and my voice is filled with gentleness, and meekness and pride does not have a place in our home. We walk in unity, humbleness and love for one another every day. In Jesus' name, Amen.

Seven

"Popularity has nothing to do with how many friends you have. It has everything to do with how truthful, loyal, and committed you are to your friendship."

The Inner Circle: Choosing Your Friends Wisely

Friends are a key factor in each of our lives. Friends are there when we are up, when we are down, and to fellowship and hang out with from time to time. There are some friends that you may talk to every day and some that you may see or speak to every six or seven months and you are able to pick back up with them as if you just spoke with them the day before. Nonetheless, you know who your true friends are. I have a couple of friends, Vicki and Terricinia, who I may see or talk to every few months, yet when we see each other, it is as if, we never missed a beat. Yet, we understand that we have a true and loyal friendship.

Overall, it is always good to choose your friends wisely. We have often heard the phrase "true friends are hard to come by." What a true statement. It has been said that marrying your best friend makes the best spouse. I can certainly say that Micheal is my best friend and we understand what it takes to have a God-marriage. Meaning, we place God at the head of our marriage and we seek Him as our mutual Best Friend. We can totally depend on each other or we can choose to totally trust and depend on God. After all, He is the One who has created us and knows every fiber of our being, so wouldn't that make Him the authority on how to teach us how to treat and love one another? Absolutely!

There are biblical examples of healthy relationships and not so healthy relationships that show us what it takes to endure and adjust to things in everyday life. Ruth and Naomi had a very committed and loyal relationship. Ruth was the daughter-in-law to Naomi. Because of Ruth's love for Naomi she refused to leave her after their husbands died. Naomi wanted Ruth and her other daughter-in-law Orpah to go back to their families for support. Orpah went back to her family and Ruth was committed and insisted on staying with Naomi.

She proved to be a very good friend and she valued Naomi's opinion concerning Boaz and they remained true to one another. Naomi did not have to help Ruth develop a relationship with Boaz. Remember, she was her late son, Mahlon's widow. Here was an example of true love and understanding that Ruth was still young enough to carry on with her life. The love she had for her daughter-in-law was a "selfless" kind of love. Just imagine for a moment when your mother-in-law instructs you to get cleaned up and put on your best perfume and go out and meet a man that you have known for a very short time and when he falls asleep lie at his feet. Ruth had to really trust Naomi to be obedient and do the very thing she instructed her to do.

In Ruth's case it was not about her needs or desires, but about being a help, a blessing to her mother-in-law. She was willing to do what the Lord required of her, love, honor and respect her mother-in-law. God honors us when we respect those in authority over us. Boaz was an honorable man. He not only had respect for Naomi, but for Ruth. She was patient and ready when it was her season to marry. She had confirmation through Ruth. When the time was right, it was done in an orderly and respectful manner. If Naomi had said to her it is not your time, I believe Ruth would have respected her wisdom and waited.

Sometimes God says wait, it is not our season and we tend to want to hurry a situation or pretend we didn't hear His voice. This causes us to move too quickly and we later regret that we did not heed to the voice of God. When it comes to a mate God does not give you a blemished ram, if you will; He gives you His very best. He is not a God of leftovers when it comes to creation. However, He is a God that will give you a fresh start, just like Ruth. In biblical times, when offerings were given to the Lord the best fatted calf was given, not the skinny, blemished weakling. Now, if you have a small husband, I am not saying that isn't God's best for you. How many of you know that some of the best gifts come in small packages.

Now, Ruth could have said this is a crazy old woman and I will not embarrass myself by doing what she is telling me to do. Her disobedience would have caused a change in the plan God had for her and she would have missed out on every blessed promise of God. Ruth married Boaz and conceived a baby boy named Obed. Because of Naomi's wisdom and instruction to Ruth she was able to receive the blessing of Obed. She loved and cared for him as though he were her very own. All that Naomi and Ruth endured was a part of God's plan; a plan that changed the course of biblical history. Through this history we know that Obed was the father of Jesse, and Jesse was the father of David, who would later become king of Israel.

I am often reminded of my own mother-in-law, Geraldine, who I affectionately, call my mother- in- love because she is a wonderful friend and there is nothing that I would not do for her. We can talk about anything and we have great admiration and respect for one another. More importantly, we share a common bond, her son, my husband, Micheal. I understood early on in our marriage that his Mother is his "Sunshine" and that he is her "one and only son". So many times you hear of horror stories of women who do not get along with their mother-in-law and how they do not have a relationship with them. Can you imagine the tension that it must bring on a marriage?

There are some people that believe that if they have a lot of friends that they are secure and happy with that, whether the friends are loyal or not. Many will say they are loyal friends, but who can find one that is truly reliable? (Proverbs 20:6) If I have not but one friend that is loyal and committed to our friendship I render that priceless. I'd rather have that one than to have a few that cannot be trusted. Friends are a dime a dozen, it is okay to have a half dozen worth of them.

Have you ever had a friend that is always willing to give advice on relationships and she is ever so willing to tell her girlfriends on what to do with "their" man? However, looking back, she is not in a steady relationship, marriage, or all her exes live in Texas! Truly she is not an authority to give advice on relationships. Friends are great to have, but you want to make sure that there are boundaries set. A friend knows their boundaries and they dare not cross them. For instance, no matter how close you may be with your girlfriend, your relationship with your husband should never be the topic of discussion when it comes to personal matters. In that instance, your husband is your best friend. Friends may mean well, but they may not have your best interest at heart.

Jesus had twelve disciples, yet He had three that were in His inner circle. There should be very few people who are in your "inner circle". Having your husband as your best friend, you both understand that what happens between you, stays between you. The last thing you want to see is you revealing your most intimate details to your girlfriend and to have what you have shared with her to back fire and she capitalizes on your weak moments and uses that as her strength to get closer to your husband. It happens every day when that so-called friend turns into a frenemy.

I have had conversations in the past with older women who do not believe that a married woman should be friends with a single woman. I believe, however, that it is possible to be a married woman and have single friends, however, I also believe that because you are a married woman you have an obligation to your husband and family and hanging out like you are a single woman is totally inappropriate. I am not saying that you can't go out for lunch or shopping together, but just hanging out at all times of the night is not what a virtuous woman does. It is healthy to have another married couple of like precious faith that you and your husband socialize with. Fellowshipping and having a couple's night out can do wonders when trying to relax from a tough work week.

It is also imperative that your husband has friends that he can fellowship with on his own as well. I love spending time with my husband, however, we understand that we need time apart to miss one another. Believe and know that you have complete support and trust for one another. So much so, that you love each other on purpose… no matter what. If your husband is your best friend make it a habit to spend quality time together.

It usually takes twenty-one days to form a habit. So for twenty-one days make a point to do one thing that is just for the two of you. For example, a date night once a week, or writing love notes, giving each other massages, or bath time together. If your finances do not call for a vacation away on an island, then plan a staycation. Your husband is not the enemy. Remember, we wrestle against powers, principalities, rulers of darkness and wickedness in high places. The real enemy is Satan and he can use your husband, friends, as well as, family to try and cause division in your marriage.

As I mentioned earlier, words have power and we should surround ourselves with friends that walk in truth and integrity. A friend that understands truth and is not afraid of it, is a friend indeed. A friend speaks into your life and they are not afraid to tell you the truth, even if it hurts. Friends edify and encourage you in the right things of God. We do not however, have to receive negativity, doubt or fear from someone that we deem as a friend.

Jezebel was not a good example of a friend. She was conniving and behaved contrary to the Word of God. Jezebel was a selfish manipulator without a conscience. To add insult to injury, she plotted murders against the servants of God. I would liken her by today's standards, a female crime boss. She was wicked by every sense of the word. A woman that was without a doubt, wicked to the core and not worthy of being a friend.

God is a jealous God. Exodus 20:5 says *"I the LORD God, am a jealous God who will not share your affections with any other god!"* Worshipping another person, including your husband, is not wise. A woman of influence and a good example of loyalty was Esther. She was a woman of faith and prayer. Her husband, king Xerxes, had favor with God because of Esther. A man that finds a wife finds a good thing, and obtains favor from the Lord. Esther was able to save the king and the Jews because of her friendship and relationship with her cousin Mordecai. He was able to get to her and warn her about the dangers that lie ahead. Esther was able to expose Haman, the enemy. God placed Mordecai at the right place at the right time.

God knew that Esther would need favor from the king to save her people, the Jews.

Esther led the Jews on a fast that would forever change the course of their lives literally. Esther was full of wisdom and obedient, so much so, God gave her favor with the king! Although Xerxes was the king, as well as, her husband, Esther did not put him on a pedestal as I would imagine many had done. She recognized the importance of her loyalty to God. Is there an Esther or Jezebel in your inner circle? Are they loyal and will do whatever it takes to show it, or are they like Jezebel, self-centered and evil? It has been said "If you want to know what you look like, look at your friends." That is a good indication of where you are going and who's going with you. Selfish gain never prospers in the end, however, loyalty clothed with trust and integrity does. There is a great reward in genuine friendship built off of trust and loyalty that will carry you through a lifetime. There is a friend that is loyal no matter what. *Greater love has no one than this, to lay down one's life for his friends. (John 15:13 NKJV)* Jesus loved us enough to lay down His life for us. If there were a friend we would choose, it would be with Him. We can go to Him and share what's on our heart, without pre-judgment or condemnation. We can share our most intimate secrets and we do not have to be concerned with it going any further. What a testament when we can have that kind of ultimate friendship.

I have very few friends that I have in my inner circle. There have been people who have tried to befriend me and I soon discovered what their true motives were and I had to make the decision to love them from a distance. Women can be very complex at times. If I can be real here, sometimes women can be jealous and jealous for many reasons. It can be something as simple as, the way that you dress and they may be insecure in who they are and feel intimidated. When you know who and whose you are there is no need to feel intimidated by another woman. We as women have enough to deal with on a daily basis than to concentrate on what another woman is or is not doing. God has created us fearfully and wonderfully. We are created in His image and likeness.

There should never be a time that we allow jealousy, and low self-esteem filter into our hearts and our thought process. Because of jealousy and rebellion Haman wanted to be king and Satan wanted to be God. They both were stripped from their positions of authority. If they both had focused on their own uniqueness they would have realized that they did not need to try and covet positions that were not for them. If you are that person that feels like you are not worthy or you want to be someone that you are not, give it to the Lord. Begin to thank Him where you are for being worthy of what He has destined for your life.

Just like each person has their own finger print that is unique and not like anyone else. God has intentionally made each of us unique in our own right. We as women of God need to walk with confidence that we are here to encourage and lift one another up. I am a firm believer in rejoicing when something wonderful happens to someone. Why bother being envious of what God has done in the life of someone else? That is a waste of time and energy that can be used to celebrate the uniqueness and gifts of other women.

Rules of thumb to live by:

1. *Choose your friends wisely. There should be very few friends in your inner circle*
2. *When choosing your friends, know there should never be a time to discuss your husband or marriage*
3. *Learn to make your husband your best friend and agree to keep private what happens between you just between you*

Prayer

Father, thank you for showing me how to discern and choose my friends wisely. Help me to be that loyal, trustworthy, and dependable friend You have called me to be. I decree and declare that I am an example of how a godly woman lives and I want to represent you well. I surrender all fears and any insecurities that I may have. I walk with confidence, integrity and a love that is representative of who You are.

In Jesus' name, Amen.

Eight

I will praise You, for I am fearfully and wonderfully made; Marvelous are Your works, and that my soul knows very well. Psalm 139:14

Know Your Identity: You Are Who God says You Are

When we focus on what others think of us then that means we are not focused on who God says we are. We live in a time where bullying and labeling are common place. When others speak into our lives and they resort to name calling, our fleshly body wants to react. We have to know and understand that God has made each one of us special in His sight and it should not matter what others think or say. From the time of our existence and the time that we were conceived in the womb of our mother, God spoke into our very existence and called us by name.

How magnificent is that? God spoke into our spirit and said what we would be and what His divine purpose was for our lives. God speaks a thing and there it is, manifested for all to see His glory!

We encounter different types of people in our lifetime. Many will be confident in who they are and there will be some who will have low self-esteem. It is important to understand that God does not make mistakes. He created each of us the way that He wanted. We begin to understand that our creation was an act of love. He thought about us, loves us without condition and will never leave or forsake us. If He has taken the time to literally think about every detail and fiber of our being, wouldn't that make us special to Him? Thoughtful planning and proper care was taken when our journey began from our Mother's womb and into the world we now call home.

Our life is a like a puzzle. We can have all the pieces, but the puzzle is put into place one piece at a time. Whatever God spoke into our existence, He gives it to us one piece at a time. Think about it, could we possibly handle knowing everything He has planned for us here on the earth? From the day you were born, until the day comes when you go on to glory. It would be too much information to handle causing our minds to go into overload. Some would be overly confident and a lover of themselves. God just wants us to utilize whatever gifts He has placed in us and to give

Him the glory for it. It is our reasonable service to seek His face and listen for what piece of the puzzle is the next piece that will bring our destiny that much closer to where He wants us.

It is easy to lose our identity when we become one with our husband. I remember talking to my friend Karen B. one day. She was going through a divorce and she said something that I could relate to. She said "I can now go to the grocery store and actually get the ice cream that I like and buy whatever I want." Meaning, she didn't have to shop based on what her husband wanted or liked. We lose so much of our identity trying to please our husband, sacrificing at times, what we want or like. We forget about the Father, oftentimes putting Him on the back burner because we have made our husbands that thing we put on a pedestal.

When we begin to see ourselves just as God sees us, we then begin to put our focus in the right place. In order to love ourselves and know our identity, we must first know who Christ is, He is our Advocate, our Guide and Director of our life. I mentioned earlier about the uniqueness of the finger print. Well, we can begin to see ourselves as individuals that God labels as His own. We are joint heirs with Jesus. So that means we have the same blood-bought rights and privileges as Jesus. Our faith level should be at a high simply because we have been given access to the throne! We are children of the Most High King! We represent Him and we as women should represent Him well. He has given us everything we need. No matter where we are, favor belongs to us!

But now, thus says the Lord, who created you O Jacob and He who formed you O Israel; I have called you by name; You are mine When you pass through the waters, I will be with you; And through the rivers, they shall not overflow you. When you walk through the fire, you shall not be burned. Nor shall the flame scorch you. For I am the Lord your God, The Holy One of Israel, your Savior; I gave Egypt for your ransom, Ethiopia and Seba in your place. Since you were precious in My sight, You have been honored, And I have loved you; Therefore I will give men for you, And people for your life. Fear not, for I am with you; I will bring descendants from the east, And gather you from the west; I will say to the north, 'Give them up!' And to the south, 'Do not keep them back!' Bring My sons from afar, And My daughters from the ends of the earth-Everyone who is called by name, Whom I have created for my glory; I have formed him, yes, I have made him' (Isaiah 43:1-7 NKJV). You see, it doesn't matter what others say about you, it matters what God says about you. You are His, and no weapon formed against you will prosper. You are under His mighty hand, and you are protected against the wiles of the enemy.

Labeling others seems to be the norm today. There are children that are labeled everyday by others and it has an adverse effect on them socially. Several years ago, as a teacher, I remember at the beginning of the year, we would get student evaluations. As teachers we would get the evaluations describing the incoming student and certain characteristics and behavior. As I began to read them, I noticed that some students were labeled as trouble makers, or unable to get along with other students. After a couple of years, I began to see a pattern and realized that in some cases there was a personality conflict with the student and that particular teacher. I made a conscientious decision never to read another student evaluation again.

It was then that I asked the Lord to let me see that student the way that He saw them. "Lord, allow me to see each student through Your eyes that I may not label them based off of someone else's opinion. That any student coming into my class for the new school year would be given the same equal opportunity to show who they were without pre-judgment from me." I actually found that also having the heart and the love of Christ made a difference in the life of a child. We are exactly who God says we are. We all have differences, yet there is room enough to share the love of our Father, who continues to love us without conditions.

When we are given a name by our parents, a name that was given some thought throughout our life, our name is what we are called by. No matter what condition or state we find ourselves, we know who we are because we have heard our name all of our lives. Never allow the words of another person to label you and make you feel as though you do not matter. When someone takes pleasure in trying to make your life miserable, that is usually a reflection of how they feel about themselves. It is a way to get the focus off them and on to you. Low self-esteem seems to be an issue that some women live with and if they know who they are, they do not have to accept that. Learn to love yourself because God loves every bit of you that He has created.

Throughout the years I have heard stories of how some women were treated like objects or property. The husband would belittle, demean, and antagonize the wife with com-ments like: "Look at you, who is going to want you? "Who wants a woman with kids?" Most often she is called outside of her name. I once was told in the past "I hope you fall flat on your face, when you do get married again, the man you marry will beat you". Mind you, the person that said that to me was being used by Satan to get me off. He wanted me to feel that I wasn't valuable enough to be loved. Let me tell you, the devil is a liar! God blessed me with a man that is after God's heart, and loves me unconditionally. He treats me like a queen, and I am grateful to God every day.

Many years ago, during the fifties and sixties, women were often homemakers and their husband was the bread winner. That meant that usually the wife did not have a skill and depended totally on her husband. If she ever thought about leaving, where would she go and how would she survive and support herself financially? Sadly, most women stayed even if it meant that they were unhappy. Oftentimes, enduring mental, verbal, and sometimes, physical abuse. I am, by no means, encouraging a woman to stay and endure any form of abuse. That is not God's perfect will for your life. God loves you and wants His very best for you. Living with any form of abuse can dampen your self-esteem and make you feel unworthy of love. That is another tactic of the enemy. He works on your mind to get you off God's purpose and destiny for your life. God is more powerful than the enemy. You are loved and created for His purpose. No man can dictate or determine the outcome that God has planned for your life.

Because we know who we are in Christ, we are able to let them know that God loves us just the way that we are. He created us special and He makes no mistakes and He loves us in spite of our flaws. You make a confession and say *"Lord I declare and decree, I am created in Your image and likeness. I walk with my head up knowing that I am an heir to Your kingdom and I am only who You say I am and I walk in victory every day!"* Confession is a wonderful way to express your faith in the Father.

When you ask the Father anything in Jesus' name believe it and you shall receive it. How we feel about ourselves starts with our mindset. The enemy will try and convince you that you are not good enough and that whatever you do will fail. The moment that thought enters into your mind, immediately eradicate it. Death and life are in the power of the tongue, and they that love it shall eat the fruit thereof. (Proverbs 21:23) Your thoughts of yourself should not be based off of what others think of you. Celebrate who the Father says you are, you are not a mistake, but a miracle manifested for His glory!

Prayer

Lord, today is the day that I will celebrate who you say that I am. Thank you that I walk like You and that I represent You well. I will treat others in the way that is pleasing to You. I know that as a man thinks, so is he. I know that I am a woman after Your heart and that I am an example that will lead others to know who You are. As a joint heir, I have a blood-bought right to exist, and I know that You loved me enough to call me by name. I am grateful that I am who You say that I am.
In Jesus' name, Amen.

Nine

God first above all else, virtue always, values forever

The Dynamics of a God-Wife

We have to get to a place where we have to be the example and set the standard of what the perfect wife should be. If we can be realist, we know that there is not a perfect wife. However, that does not mean that we should not try to raise the standard and strive to be as close as possible. I believe that there are godly steps that will show us how to be the wife that your husband desires and the wife he will be ultimately be pleased with. The God-wife places God first above all else, including her husband. *"A capable, intelligent, and virtuous woman-who is he who can find her? She is more precious than jewels and her value is far above rubies or pearls" (Proverbs 31:10 AMP).*

The God-wife is valuable to her husband and she is highly respected. She is confident in who she is and has no worries concerning her family. It is so important to keep ourselves in the position of ever learning. We as wives should never become complacent and not educate ourselves in the way of the Lord. Our prayer life, our praise and worship are vital to the growth and knowledge of where God is taking us. Your husband should be confident in knowing that because of your relationship with the Father, he trusts you without doubt. He knows that you walk in the ways of God and that because of your obedience to the Lord, he is blessed indeed.

I can remember when I met my husband it was important to me that I established with him a standard. I wanted Micheal to know and understand that my relationship with God was not only serious, but important. I had gone through a divorce and then eventually dating again. I began to see that after a couple of years as a divorced woman that the dating scene hadn't changed much, but I had. I prayed to the Lord that I wanted something outside of the norm. I wanted a relationship with a godly man that understood that I wanted to wait until marriage before becoming intimate.

I actually sat down and created a list. Yes ladies, an actual handwritten list. I was specific with the Father in what I wanted in a mate. Believe it or not, it works. What you are doing is releasing into the atmosphere clear-cut desires of what you want. For instance, if you want a mate that is six feet tall, dimples, a skilled chef, a lover of family, artistic, financially stable…etc. make it very clear and specific. I was clear not to leave anything out. For me, it was important that the mate that I desired was comical because I love to laugh. He had to be family oriented. It was also important for him to have a great relationship with his mother. I already knew I was confident in who I was and I needed someone who was also confident in the Lord. I said, Lord the man I meet will understand that I want to wait for marriage. I was so grateful that Micheal understood and I knew that he was the one for me. I set a standard and believed God that He would honor my request. Ladies, it is ok to compromise, but it is never ok to settle for less than God's best for your life. We are valuable in the eyesight of the Father and He is not going to give you less than His very best for you.

As a single woman, a few years ago, I remember at my former church there was a guest apostle who called an alter call. I was there in line as he was praying and speaking prophetically to the members. When he got to me, I remember him stopping through the prayer and he said to me "I see laughter, so much laughter in your life! Then he said "You will love again!" Of course I was taken aback because he was excited as he said that to me. Let me tell you, it did not stop there. A few weeks later a Rabi was having breakfast with my then boss and former Pastor and I happened to walk in the room and I spoke to him. I noticed that he was staring at me. He apologized for the staring and continued speaking and he said "Are you in the military?" I then said no, I have never been in the military. The Rabi, then said "I don't know why, but I see the military all around you." I, once again was taken aback.

Little did I know, that what both these men spoke into my life would happen sooner than I realized. You see, that was right before Micheal had come into my life. I met Micheal and we became friends. In my head, I always thought that he would be a great match for some fortunate lady, he was just that kind of guy. God quickly reminded me of the words that were spoken by the two men of God. It was as if I had a "Golden Skillet" hit over my head moment. One, Micheal was very funny. Two, he was in the military! What are the odds of that? Needless to say, I am a firm believer that God will use people to speak into your situation and give you revelation. There were people that I could have settled for, but as I look back on it now, I would have been miserable and most likely sitting in front of a divorce attorney. I had to listen to my inner voice and know that it would not have been best for me to settle.

It was crucial that the man in my life was not stagnate in his goals and his life. In life you have to have a plan. Without a plan, you plan to fail and that was not an option for me. I believe that the enemy will try and send a counterfeit to try and thwart what God means as a genuine life partner. The counterfeit will make all kinds of promises that he has no intention of keeping. Motivation is not his strong suit. Mediocre is his middle name and you become an afterthought. You soon find out that he has no clue of his future and clueless when it comes to you. I am so thankful that God sent me a genuine man who not only knew where he was going, but knew and respected me as a person. The heart of a man does matter, especially when you are ready to give him yours. The God-wife upholds a standard and she does not waiver from it. Never negate the fact that Holy Spirit is there whenever you need Him. He never lies and He is faithful and full of wisdom. He is a very reliable source who can be trusted at all times.

The God-wife is diligent. She is, by no means lazy concerning her household. She is consistent with her prayer life and the wellbeing of her family. God created the wife as a help-meet for her husband. What exactly is a "help-meet" you might ask? Well, that is a title that is not taken lightly, but considered an honor. You, God-wife, are worthy of the calling to be that assistant, helper, a good steward of everything that your husband needs.

At the same time, you and your husband are equal partners and no one role is greater than the other. Your husband depends on you to take care of him and to know that your home is a safe haven for him and your family. You, as a wife, understand that your husband is the protector and the driving force as a man of God for the family. There is a balance, not to be twisted with a dictatorship, where the husband is the "controller" and rules with an "iron fist", if you will.

Many households have an agreement as to who handles the finances, does the shopping and so on. If your husband is better at handling the finances, then by all means, let him handle it. If you on the other hand are a whiz with the finances, then you should handle it. As long as there is an agreed balance, concerning responsibilities, then there is peace in the home. A God-wife takes care of herself. We as women can get caught up with the issues of everyday. We can easily neglect ourselves. Not only should we maintain a household, but take pleasure and care in making sure we are in shape spiritually and physically. Our spiritual body needs daily nourishment with the Word and prayer. This is where our spirit body can grow and mature in the things of the Lord. Physical endurance is just as important because we have to be able to work, manage our home, finances and still be there for our husband.

There is often a misconception that if a woman does not work, she lives a life of leisure. This could not be further from the truth. I have been a stay at home wife since 2010. I no longer have to punch a physical time clock and report outside of my home to an office building filled with co-workers and a boss. I am my own boss and I report to my CEO, Micheal Young. My day actually starts between 4:30 AM and 5:00 AM every morning. As I mentioned earlier, I get up and prepare breakfast and lunch for my husband. By the time he leaves for work at 5:45 AM, I do not have the luxury of going back to bed. By the way, did I mention that Micheal and I have been raising our four year old grandson? We have been afforded the opportunity to raise Jailen from birth.

When I came off my job in 2010, I had no idea that in 2011, we would be raising a newborn. God has a way of setting us up and we have no idea until the actual manifestation. We serve an all-knowing God. He knew that Jailen would be a major part of our lives. To make a long story short, we have been blessed and our daughter Lauren, against all odds, has been able to complete college with high honors on time. She was also able to graduate from Law School and is now preparing for the South Carolina Bar. To God be the glory! When we are faithful, He is faithful.

As a God-wife we wear many hats. Once my husband leaves for work I am still responsible for getting Jailen's breakfast and his school clothes ready. I then take him to school and pick him up in the afternoon. Because I am a woman of a certain age (forty-eight to be exact) I imagined that my husband and I would have an empty nest.

However, God had a different plan. Sacrifices are often made in life, and we really haven't lived unless a sacrifice has been made. Regular chores and errands have become my norm. I prepare dinner, assist with and check homework every night. Yes, my four year old grandson has homework. My day usually ends about 11 PM or 12 AM. My day starts again the next morning at 4:30 to 5:00 AM. So, you see, it is not all a life of leisure because I no longer work outside of the home, but a life of purpose.

I sometimes have to pull double duty, if you will. I am clearly no saint, but I am able to balance out my day as a God-wife, simply because God is my Director. The God-wife prepares consistently for her family. Meals, laundry, and extracurricular activities. She makes herself available as well as, flexible to the needs of her husband. Now, I have encountered women who work every day outside of the home. They will easily say "I don't have time to cook, or I clean my house whenever I can." Please understand, I am not knocking that, however, always remember, there is a woman that will do the things that you aren't willing to do for your husband. Trust me, there are women who are willing to cook and bring your husband her "special" dish to work and share her unofficial culinary skills with him.

There are creative and easy ways to make meals happen. One pot or crock pot meals are convenient ways to pre-pare lunch or dinner. These can be planned and prepared ahead of time. Perhaps preparing enough to last a few days. This process may be a good idea to cook on a Saturday or Sunday (usually off days for most) for meals during the week. This takes the pressure off of you to cook when you get off of work. These meals can also be prepared and frozen and used for a later date. The God-wife never fails to prepare for the future.

As a woman, I like to shop, however, I do not find it hard to save to help keep finances in check. It is vital to be a good steward over what God blesses us with financially. Saving for a rainy day is always wise. Once again, sacrifices have to be made in order to accomplish a goal. I have met women who love spending their time on the phone gossiping and they make it their business to keep up with the happenings of others.

A God-wife, spends her time wisely. She doesn't have time for idle gossip. Proverbs 31: 27 (AMP) says, "*She looks well to her household and the bread of idleness (gossip, discontentment, and self-pity) she will not eat*". This is a crucial mistake and it leaves little to be desired in a God-wife. We want to set the example and exemplify excellence in all that we do. Good character is priceless, and should be valued and protected at all cost. "*Many daughters have done virtuously, nobly, and well [with the strength of character that is steadfast in goodness], but you excel them all*" (*Proverbs 31:29 AMP*).

There will be days when I do not feel my absolute best. The day does not stop because my body may not be at its best. I have to know what I can handle in the course of the day, yet use wisdom enough to know my body needs proper rest. Sometimes we try to be everything to everyone else, and we can easily forget to take proper care of ourselves. We have to understand that when our body is giving us a warning that something isn't quite right, we need to take heed, learn to monitor and adjust to our situation.

No matter where we are in our lives, there is always someone watching. People have a tendency to forget all the wonderful things we may have done, but somehow they like to remember the mistakes we made along the way. It is vital that we lead with integrity and continue to have a character that is pleasing to our Father. The God-wife knows and understands that her walk should be a positive reflection of her husband. No wife, or potential wife wants to be a disappointment or an embarrassment to her family, especially to her husband or the man she is about to marry.

The God-wife considers it a privilege to be a ray of light representing her husband. She is confident in knowing that all her efforts are not in vain. Your relationship with your husband brings glory to God. We have to operate our marriage as a partnership. God is the CCIC (Chief Creator in Charge) and we are partners with Him. His example is the best example. The last time I checked God does not make mistakes, we do. That is exactly why He is God. He guides us through whatever mistakes we make and because of grace, He does not hold it over our heads. His grace and mercy are sufficient. What a beautiful place to be, when we, His children, reap the benefits of His unfailing love.

The God-wife loves in sickness and in health. We all have hopes of living a long healthy life with our spouse. However, with the changes in life, health issues happen. In such cases, we need to know how to pray and walk by faith and not by sight. We need to be ready at all times to wield the sword of our faith. I remember one day, a few years ago, when I still worked, I received a phone call from the Naval Hospital in Portsmouth. The voice on the phone had called to tell me that Micheal was rushed to the hospital. I immediately went into a panic because the person was being very vague and was not giving me the information I needed on the phone. The only thing they could tell me was that whatever happened was enough to admit him. I made the necessary arrangements to leave and go to the hospital.

Once I got there, I saw my husband on the bed with all types of cords and monitors attached to him. Finally, I was able to get some answers from the doctor and the nurse. Apparently they thought that Micheal had a heart attack. They had him hooked to the monitor checking his heart. In my mind how is this possible? My husband was only thirty-six years old and healthy, so I thought. Well, it turns out that they discovered that his blood sugar level was off the charts and his A1C was a 13! Prior to this, I had no idea what A1C meant. What I learned was that a normal A1C on average is about a 5. So Micheal was well above the normal range.

It was still early in our marriage and I had not anticipated anything like this to happen. This is where your faith is really tested. We hear the vows "In sickness and in health" but do we really take the time to think about how poignant those words are? If I can honestly answer that, I would have to say no. I had the responsibility of calling Micheal's mother in Mississippi to tell her that her only son was just admitted to the hospital. That was one of the hardest things I had to do. In life things happen unexpectedly, however, we have to know what verse of scripture to stand on. A prayer life is so critical especially when we have life issues staring us in the face, so to speak. We were able to get through it and Micheal was on his way to better health with the proper diet and medication.

How do you handle sudden life hiccups? Do you go into a sudden panic or do you allow Holy Spirit to give you calm as you stand on the Word of God? Always remember that God specializes in the supernatural and when it looks bleak and impossible, God is there to get you through. I tend to believe the report of the Lord, not the negativity that the enemy tries to embed in my head. God is able to give us help in the time of trouble. Go to God in the throne of grace and pray over yourself, your husband, and family. I Timothy 1:2 says, *"May God our Father and Jesus our Lord show you His kindness and mercy and give you great peace of heart and mind" (TLB).*

Prayer

Father, thank you that Holy Spirit is there to be the calm during unexpected life issues. I stand on Your Word and believe every written blessed promise. I walk with assurance knowing that as a God-wife, I am a positive refection of my husband and complete representation of You. I understand that because of You, I am in a beautiful place. Thank you that I am able to maintain my household under Your guidance and I am able to grow and mature in the things of You.

In Jesus' name, Amen.

Ten

So Jesus said to them, "Because of your unbelief; for assuredly, I say to you, if you have faith as a mustard seed, you will say to the mountain, Move from here to there, and it will move; and nothing will be impossible for you." (Matthew 17:20 NKJV)

Nothing is Too Hot for God

Fire can be defined as: The state or form of combustion that is manifested in light flame and heat: something burning the fire in the furnace; something resembling fire in its brilliance heat, intense feeling or enthusiasm; an intense suffering; severe trial or ordeal; to cause to glow or shine. We begin to respond or be excited when the fire comes. A wonderful example of enduring the fire and flames, is when Daniel and the Hebrew boys were in the fiery furnace. They had no need for caution. They knew that God would intervene and get them through it. Can you imagine the excitement of knowing that if God be for you, who can be against you? He intervened and Daniel and the Hebrew boys were not burned! No weapon formed against us shall prosper. How amazing is that! Listen ladies, when the fire gets hotter, PRAISE HARDER!!!

As women, we are sometimes faced with things that tend to stress us out and leave us tired and discouraged. The people on your job and in your family, can seemingly work on your last nerve. It seems like if it is not one thing, it is another. As women, we were created to multi task. We are by nature nurturers, so we want to fix everything, especially when it comes to our husbands. Sometimes the fire seems too hot to bear. God is on the verge of releasing you out of the flames. You may be tried by the fire, but you are inspired. In larger cities for fire safety, there is something called a fire escape. Webster's defines a fire escape as: fire-proof stairway down an outside wall to help people escape from a burning building.

Isaiah 43:15-19 states, *"I am the LORD Your Holy One, The Creator of Israel your King. Thus says the Lord who makes a way in the sea and a path through the mighty waters. Who brings forth the chariot and the horse, the army, and the power (They shall lie together and not rise; they are extinguished, they are quenched like a wick!) Do not remember the former things, nor, consider the things of old. Behold I will do a new thing, Now it shall spring forth; shall you not know it? I will even make a road in the wilderness and rivers in the desert.*" We all have heard of a fire extinguisher and what it is used for. It is a portable device containing chemicals that can be sprayed on a fire to put it out. God is not only our fire escape, but He is also our extinguisher!

A fire guard is another form of protection. It is used to keep the fire from burning you. *"When my spirit was over-whelmed within me, then You knew my path. In the way in which I walk, they secretly set a snare for me. Look on my right hand and see, for there is no one that acknowledges me; Refuge has failed me; no one cares for my soul. I cried out to You, O Lord; I said, You are my refuge; my portion in the land of the living"* (Psalm 142: 3-5).

Fire clay is something capable of resisting intense heat used for making firebricks. As we know, God is the potter and we are the clay. He has created us to withstand the heat. The enemy would have you to be firewood which is the wood used for fuel. It is Satan's purpose to destroy our destiny and steer us in the wrong direction. But God has given us the ability to set up firing squads and take out the enemy in one shot! We have not been given the spirit of fear, but the spirit of love and a sound mind; that being the mind of Christ! Hebrews 12:29 makes it very clear when it says, "For our God is a consuming fire." Consume means: to destroy, to do away with, to use up, to drink, devour, absorb completely engross or obsess. Who are we to believe that God will not protect us? God is able to devour up what tries to devour us. As wives, we are in a wonderful place because we belong to God and there is nothing that God will not do for us, when we are walking upright before Him.

Allow God to completely absorb that which is trying to devour you. Finances, people, or things. In some cases, it may seem like your husband is demanding and you can't handle the heat he may be giving out. There is no situation too hot for God. As a God-wife, we have to get out of the way and allow God do what He does best. Trust me, He can handle it! I want you to know that when things get too hot, be encouraged in knowing that God is there for your way of escape. Women are special to God and we are blessed to know that we have a heavenly Father that loves and cares enough to rescue us from the heat of life.

God's purpose is not to destroy us but to restore us. The enemy is the destroyer (fire flame) but God has promised to restore the things the enemy tries to take from our lives. All the times of frustrations and defeat; all the moments of regret; all the pains of lost opportunities; all the hurts of a broken relationship can be healed through God, the Father. The marriage covenant is always at risk for the enemy to try and divide and conquer what God has joined together. God-wife, God is building His kingdom within you, a kingdom of love, peace, righteousness, victory, redemption and a right relationship with not only God, but your husband. Remember, when things get tough, heartache and discouragement are only for a moment, but peace and joy are everlasting. Brighter days are ahead, so trust that God is a lover of covenant and that you and your husband will take joy in knowing that no matter how hot it gets, God can withstand the heat and bring you through triumphantly!

There will be times when you and your husband are believing God for something and it looks impossible. However, with faith, you are able to stand in unity and see it happen right before your eyes. We can't always share what we are going through or what we are believing God for because everyone will not rejoice with you. That is why your husband is your best friend and confidant and the two of you can walk in agreement by faith. Together you can extinguish the wiles (flames) of the enemy, allowing you both the ability to have the victory through the course of your marriage.

Prayer

Father, I come boldly to Your throne of grace, believing that You are the Protector from the fiery flames of the enemy. I decree and declare Psalms 91 over my marriage. I know that there is nothing too hard for You Lord. Thank you that I am not intimidated by the enemy. I have been given by

You Lord, the authority to put the enemy on notice, that he has no power or authority over me, my husband, or our marriage. The enemy is a defeated foe and we walk triumphantly together as a team.

In Jesus' name, Amen.

Eleven

"Love is like a bright light at the end of the tunnel, it is reachable, you know it is coming, and you are going to get there."

Note to the Single Ladies: Walk in Your Divine Wholeness

There is a spiritual war going on and the enemy has a hit out on women that are trusting and believing God for that godly man and priest for their life. Now is the time to trust and believe God like never before. God honors His Word. Therefore, He cannot lie…His Word is true. The peace of God makes you whole, not a man. Choosing a mate for your life is serious and should not be taken lightly. I mentioned earlier that I was very specific in what I believed God for in a husband. There is great power when you believe and pray. God knows what we need before we ask; remember He is omnipotent (all knowing). Some people actually believe that it takes another to "complete" them. That could not be further from the truth.

We must first have to have a complete relationship in Christ. Quality time with the Father is necessary. It is then that you are able to hear clearly what He is saying for you in your life. Always trust God for strength in your time of temptation and weakness. Trust me, temptations will come, remember Jesus was also tempted by Satan and He stood on the Word. Always pray the Word, it works! When the enemy comes in, like a flood the Spirit of the Lord will lift up a standard against him. In your singleness, the devil is fighting a losing battle with God on your side. He is already defeated. There is great power when you believe and pray. Use the authority given to you by the power of God. I spoke earlier about your confessions when believing for a mate. Believe that the manifestation of your desires will happen through your confession of faith.

There is something that I discovered, a revelation, if you will, that when you make your list of what you desire from God in a mate, make one for your mate. Just imagine that you put down all that you would do to honor your future husband and present it to the Lord. It is now in the atmosphere and your future husband is believing God for the same thing that you have written down for yourself to honor him. Now there are two prayers that are in the atmosphere and because you both were specific in your desires, God has honored you both and now you both have been strategically placed together by Him. A Strategic and consistent prayer life brings about results.

We can pray the same prayer all day every day, however, when we tell the Father what we desire, for example, *God, I want a mate that attends church with me every Sunday.* Now, it is good that you want a mate that attends church every Sunday, however, you are more specific when you say," *God, thank you that my future husband loves You with his whole heart and he will love me like Christ loves the church. He will attend church every Sunday and become an active member in ministry."* Do you see the difference? We have to have a plan in mind of what we want and make it clear to the Father when we pray. Fall in Love with Jesus and value the relationship with Him. God will honor that and give you the desires of your heart.

Ascribe to the Lord the glory due His name. Bring an offering and come before Him; worship the Lord in the splendor of His holiness. The very best thing that we can offer to the Lord is to love Him with our whole heart. I have been in conversations with single women and they all seem to have the same frustrations…there just aren't any good men out there. I make it very clear that there are good men, who love the Lord and will love them, as well as, commit to them. Men will go as far as you allow them.

Women do not realize the power that they have when it comes to relationships.

I married the first time at the early age of twenty. Too young to know what on earth to do with a husband. However, I learned along the way. Today, I believe I would have waited and allowed myself to at least live on my own before committing and living with a husband. I literally went from my parent's house right into a marriage. I did not know what it was like to live on my own until my divorce in 2006. It was then that I was in the single mom category with two teenage children. My life, as I knew it, took a drastic change that I had to come to terms with. When you get married you never see yourself one day as a divorcee'. As we all know life happens and we have to be ready to tackle the transitions. *"You have made known to me the path of life; You will fill me with joy in Your presence, with eternal pleasures at Your right hand (Psalm 16:11).*

The God that we serve is so amazing that He already has a plan for our lives. It never ceases to amaze me that we have all sorts of ideas for our life. He is the final authority on what it is that we should do. When I am asked to pray for someone I always tell them that I am going to pray that God's perfect will be done, not mine. As single women it is important to remember that you are set apart for holy use by the Father. Your body belongs to you. Never allow a man to make you feel like you need to give up what you want specifically for your future husband. I know that sounds "old fashioned". However, you are setting a standard for the kind of man you want in your life. As a matter of fact, ladies, men will respect you as you respect yourself.

Love yourself enough to know that when you love Christ first, and you have an intimate relationship with Him, God will honor your faithfulness. I mentioned earlier that temptation will come, and believe me it will. Our flesh is weak and Satan knows that. Holy Spirit is there to guide you through your temptation. Believe me when I tell you it is not easy, however, there are things that you can do to avoid temptation at all cost.

I have a very dear friend that had a dilemma a few years ago. She was attracted to a very handsome man who had just become a member of her church. She noticed that several of the other women (single and married) also had their eyes on him. My friend, who I will call Kate, (not her real name) was well educated and very attractive. She had never been married, but she was ready to find her Boaz and settle down. These other women tried everything they could to get his attention. She wanted to say something to him, but she didn't want to seem too forward. I said to her, "Kate, these women are practically throwing themselves at him, and he doesn't seem the least interested. You have an advantage over them. Just be yourself and approach him as a friend. You want to do just the opposite of what the other ladies are doing. I also told her that he was probably so used to women throwing themselves at him that he had become accustomed to the advances.

Kate was willing to be herself and allow God to do the rest. Needless to say, they built a godly friendship. I continued to encourage her to do it God's way. They eventually began to date. Kate also set boundaries with this young man. When they went out they chose not to kiss, or to get themselves in compromising situations. If he were to visit he would make a point to leave at an appropriate hour.

Needless to say, they got engaged (I was blessed and privileged to help her pick out her engagement ring) and eventually married and they are still happily married today. They decided to wait until they were married to be intimate. They wanted to make sure that their relationship was holy and acceptable in the eyes of the Lord. When God sends the right one, he will understand and accept whatever standard you set for yourself. I have met women who have made statements like "I don't need a man, I like my life. The same women that have said this to me have later admitted that they long to have someone in their life, or the first person that came into their life, they settled.

Being in a relationship just for the sake of being in a relationship is not healthy. Why sacrifice happiness for the sake of saving face of being alone. With Christ we are never alone and He loves us unconditionally, in spite of all of our flaws.

Love yourself enough to realize that settling is never an option. Forsaking Mr. Right for Mr. Right Now is not wise. Have enough wisdom to recognize when he is not that into you. When a man appears to show interest and he is always too busy to spend time with you on a regular basis it is usually a red flag and a big indication that he does not see you as a priority. Whenever there is a family function or the holidays and he finds every excuse not to attend, or better yet, he conveniently forgets to call you to tell you he can't make it. When you know your worth, you don't accept any and everything from a potential mate. The best indicator that he is in to you, is when he makes a point to call you, to pursue you earnestly. He is not excuse laden and slow to show you that he takes you seriously. Why? You have set a standard of what is acceptable and unacceptable concerning you. He does not continue to make excuses for marrying you. For example, if he says, let's hold off until my finances are in order. I want to be able to build financial stability, and marriage is not an option right now. Yes, you want be financially stable, however, that can sometimes take years to accomplish.

Are you willing to wait years for that to happen or are you willing to make that commitment and work on building a financially stable marriage together. Maybe he thinks that you should live together first to see if you are "marriage" material. That is definitely not the best indicator. When a man has found a wife in you, he is ready to commit to you for a lifetime. I know of a couple of cases where the same man that stalled to discuss marriage or commitment, married someone else within six months to a year later. It is this simple, he knows when the "one" comes into his life it just happened that you were not the "one".

A man that is worth his salt, so to speak, is not afraid to be honest with you. He appreciates the fact that you set boundaries. Being a lady is never a bad thing. It shows that you can love and respect yourself without hesitation. Demand respect and he will respect you. This should be a requirement when looking for qualities in a potential husband. Believe it or not, most men love a woman that is confident and knows exactly what she wants. Always be truthful in your relationship, you will also want the same from him. Some men actually find that very appealing.

When you walk into a room people should see confidence, and that you are secure in who you are. People should see virtue and that you are set apart for Christ's sake. I love how Esther was among other women to win the kings heart and because of her confidence and obedience, she was able to stand out among all the others. That is the place we want to find ourselves. Your ultimate goal is to be a God-wife, a woman that has the complete "planned" package

God has for your life. We want to set a standard, but not so high that your expectations are unrealistic.

Maybe you have been married before and you feel like you are done with relationships. I am a firm believer some people are in our lives for just a season and a lesson. God is a God of second chances. We should be in a place where we learn from our mistakes and move forward to the next level in our lives. In the last few years I have heard women introduce the men in their life as their fiancé, and I have asked women how long have you been engaged? I am really surprised at some of the answers I get. Some will say, a few months and others have said a few years. Some of the women have engagement rings and others did not.

Please understand, I am not knocking anyone if they do not have a ring. However, when a man knows that you are the one, he will do everything possible to make it known. He is willing to show you that he can and will commit to you. Especially when they are of a particular age they do not belabor the point. If your man presents you with an engagement ring, more than likely he doesn't have a problem with you setting a date for the wedding. I never understood a four, five, or a ten year engagement. Why? When you know that the person you have committed to is willing to spend their life with you. There are some couples that are in a relationship for companionship and they choose not to get married. However, that is not what I am speaking about. I am talking about a covenant with God between a man and woman who love one another and they want to share their lives together as husband and wife.

Ladies, it is so important to guard your heart. Proverbs 4:23 says, *"Keep your heart with all diligence, for out of it spring the issues of life."* If it is your heart's desire to be a God-wife with the God-man of your dreams, then see yourself as that. Begin to say back to God what is in His Word. Prayer is where you get faith to work. When you have a deep desire for something, it is so strong that nothing can shake what you feel. This is how the power can be released. Your faith level is at a new high and like a woman that is ready to give birth, you are ready for it to spring forth! Keep that vision board in your mind of what you desire for your future mate. Be specific with whatever you desire. *"And the desire of the righteous will be granted." Proverbs 10:24b (NKJV)*

Your thought process will take a new direction because negative thinking only gets you negative results. You want to have positive thinking so that you have positive results. That is why it is important to have positive friends around you. You want to have friends that will speak life into your situation and agree with you in prayer. A bitter, and angry friend filled with hurt is not a benefit to you when you desire to be a positive light before others. Bitterness can block the power of God releasing what He has destined for you. The enemy comes to steal, kill and destroy what God has predestined for you. Satan can't defeat you unless you allow him. There will be challenges that come along the way, however, your relationship with the Father gives you access to the throne and His favor. We all know that favor outweighs fair every time. No one can take that away, not even the enemy! The biggest fear the devil has is that you will get your breakthrough. Begin to praise God for your victory, because through Christ you already have the victory.

There are important safeguards to follow when we are walking upright before the Lord. The Word is your foundation. It is solid and with it you are on firm ground. The Word never changes. Remember, you are God's anointed and favor is your shield." *Faith comes by hearing and hearing by the Word of God (Romans 10:17).* As a woman, you must know your value. Your future husband will know your worth and he is a respecter of God and you. *"Grace and peace be multiplied to you in the knowledge* of God and of Jesus our Lord, as His divine power has given to us all things that pertain to life and godliness, through the knowledge of Him who called us by glory and virtue" 2 Peter 1:2-3 (NKJV).

Virtue can be described as character that leads to good behavior. Virtue displays wisdom, courage, kindness, good manners, courteous, modesty, generosity and self-control. When you have virtue you treat others better than you treat yourself. You make it a point to exhibit love at all times no matter how others treat you. Virtue is a part of our faith walk as women. This makes it necessary to live a life of holiness and godliness.

Being a single woman is not the end of the world. It is the beginning of a whole new world. This is the time in your life where you can enjoy your singleness until the time for you to share your life with the man God has for you. Your singleness is your time to focus on the Lord and to operate in faith. Patience is everything when it comes to having the right man in your life. We all have been guilty of being impatient and wanting what we want in life. Most often not consulting the Father on what is best for us. When in doubt seek God first before making major decisions. The best is yet to come for your life, if you believe that then you are on your way to enjoying the life that has been planned specifically for you.

Prayer

Father, thank you that as a single woman, I walk with purpose and in Your plan for my life. I am whole and complete in You Lord. I praise You Lord in advance for the victory you have already given me. I will stay in Your presence as I believe, trust, and rely on You. My desires are the desires that You have for me, and I know that Your best is my best. I make You Lord, the lover of my soul and I trust You Father completely. As I walk uprightly before You, I am patient and I believe that Your perfect will for my life is done. I am willing, ready, and able to turn to the next chapter for my life. I am a conqueror and I totally surrender my all to You Lord. I think positively for positive results. I shall have what I believe and say. I offer myself wholeheartedly to You Lord.

In Jesus' name, Amen.

Twelve

The Journey of the God-wife:
Living the Good-Life

There is a promise that has already been spoken over your life. From the very beginning of your creation you have been predestined for great things. The anointing is yours. Jesus already paid the price so that you may operate in it freely. We are able to say back to our heavenly Father what we know and believe. Some like to blame the devil for everything that happens to them. Stop giving him the credit. God deserves all the praise for what takes place in our lives. It is unfortunate that many believers focus on the enemy and how he terrorizes Christians. They don't realize how much power they are giving to him. Actually, Satan has no power. So he does not deserve any credit. Jesus never leaves or forsakes us, so in our time of trouble, He is there. Never focus on the problem, but the One who holds all the answers.

God is preparing us for our season. Being a God-wife can be a challenge, however, because of our right relationship with Him we are able to handle whatever situation we find ourselves. It is so important to make an effort to find value in yourself. Life is truly amazing because we have the victory everyday of our lives. As a God-wife, you are able to create an atmosphere that is conducive to what God has ordained for your life with your husband. He has placed the "super" to your natural and you are now operating in the supernatural. Holy Spirit works on our behalf to search the deep things of God. We have dominion wherever we go.

We are in right standing with God without feeling guilty. Remember, that the prayers of the righteous avails much power. Jesus is our Ultimate Sacrifice. He loves us and He endured for us. That is true, unfailing love that never dies. If you are single, take no thought for tomorrow; do not worry about what will make you happy today or tomorrow. Confess whatever moves your heart. God will take care of you and He will guide you in all that you do...trust Him. Jesus is the same yesterday, today and forever more. Great things will happen for you. Change your mind-set to the mind of Christ. People will try to sway you out of your salvation and the ways of God, but stand your ground. Believe that you are the righteousness of God in Christ Jesus and

that your faith cannot be moved. Go boldly and with confidence before the Lord.

Christ set the example, be a reflection of what He sees,
as if He were looking in the mirror. God-wife, God has
set the course for your destiny, now walk in it. Everything
that you have seen and experienced is not by accident. Put
away the fears and seize the opportunity that is before you.
Your destiny has been laid before the foundations of the
earth, now is the season to walk in what is in front of you.
The way has been prepared and He will lead and guide you
every step of the way. The road is clear and can be plainly
seen. Your dreams and visions are of the Lord and you are
released to go forth and birth what is inside of you. The
fire that resonates the passion within you will happen. Your
healing is a result of your faith believing that the manifestation has already taken place. Trust the Lord, and never
doubt that what He is telling you will come to pass. Speak
to your mountain with authority and watch it move out of
your way. Go forth believing that it is already done!

You can live the kingdom life right here on earth.
Remember, you are an heir and an ambassador of Christ.
When you know that your Father has your back and He has
access to everything in the earth, you are privileged. What
comfort we have when we are under His protection and
care. We walk in the promises of the Lamb of God, who
loved us enough to willingly give His life. There is no love

that can compare, not even the love of our husband. You are complete in Him, and there is no need to worry about the kind of life you will have. People will look at you and wonder how you are living well on your salary. What they do not understand is that your faith and faithfulness make it possible for you to prosper in the things of the Lord.

Favor is not fair, however it is justified. Why? Because God rewards those who diligently seek Him. He is faithful and He wants to bless you so that you may be a blessing to others. There are things in this life that we may never understand, however, God is the author and finisher of our faith, not the enemy. When the Spirit of the Lord speaks, we need to move in obedience. God will never steer us wrong concerning our life. God is there to provide every provision for our purpose. *To everything there is a season, a time for every purpose under heaven (Ecclesiastes 3:1 NKJV)* When there is a transition for our lives, everything falls into place with ease. There is no doubt or hesitation because we recognize His voice. We have often heard that life is what you make it. Life is what God gives to us to live our full potential for His glory. But it is written: *"Eyes have not seen, nor ears heard, nor has it entered into the heart of man, the things which God has prepared for those who love Him. But God has revealed them to us through His Spirit. For the Spirit searches all things, yes the deep things of God" (1 Corinthians 2:9-10 NKJV).*

Noteworthy Assessment

"Each day is a teachable moment we learn from what we have experienced and show others what to apply or not to apply in their lives."

1. **What have you experienced in your life that you are willing to show or teach others?**

2. "Think of your past as a road that leads to a detour that takes you to your intended destination…your future." **As a God-wife, what are your short-term goals? What are your long-term goals?**

3. "Life is what you make it, whatever you speak into your existence will be the evidence of what you have believed." (Hebrews 11:1) *Now faith is substance of things hoped for, the evidence of things not seen.* **What have you believed God for and it happened?**

4. *"Stop the negativity in your life and begin to surround yourself with positive thinking, speaking and actions that bring about positive results."* **What changes have you made to turn a negative into a positive?**

5. *"You know brighter days are ahead when you no longer look back and wonder if."* **What are some steps that you can take to have brighter days ahead?**

6. "Forgiveness is not an option, it is a mandate." **How hard is it for you to forgive an offense?** (Ephesians 4:32) *And be kind to one another, tenderhearted, forgiving one another, even as God in Christ forgave you.* **Have you made steps toward forgiveness?**

7. "When we are knee deep in our mess, it is with the depth of His heart that He reaches down and gets us out of it and turns our mess into our message." (John 14:1) *Let not your heart be troubled; you believe in God, believe also in Me.* **What situation in your life have you turned into your message?**

8. *"Dreams are visions that are attainable, not a wish hoping to manifest."* **What are your dreams and**

what steps have you made to accomplish them? Do you have a target date for completion?

9. "Freedom is knowing that you are no longer bound by the acceptance of others but because of grace you are truly free." (Galatians 5:1) *Stand fast therefore in liberty by which Christ has made us free, and do not be entangled again with a yoke of bondage.* **Have you learned to let people go?**

10. *"When grace covers you, fear has no place to reside." Fear is false evidence appearing real. (1 John 4:18) There is no fear in love; but perfect love cast out fear, because fear involves torment. But he who fears has not been made in perfect love.* **What have you done to release the fear and operate in the grace He has provided?**

11. *"We are all given gifts to give back to God. So don't be a hater when those who chose to use their gift or talent walk in the manifested promises of God. He is an equal opportunity God."* **Have you ever been envious or jealous of someone else's gift or talent? What things did you do to change? What are your gifts and how do you plan to utilize them?**

12. *"Life can be challenging, but how you overcome it can be very rewarding."* **How have you overcome the challenges of life? (1 John 2:13) What are your plans to stay there?**

13. *"Choose to relish in the brightness of your future, not wallow in the darkness of your past."* **As a God-wife there are things that happen and we have to let go of. What is the best way that you have found to help you move from the past?**

14. *"Take hold of the opportunities that God has gifted you. So rejoice with others when God blesses them. Begin to say to yourself, "I am next and my blessing is on the way."* **Make a list of your blessings of God. Begin to think of ways that you can bless others.**

15. *"Reflection doesn't mean to look back, it means to take in what you see then begin to make the necessary changes."* **What changes am I willing to make concerning my attitude toward my husband?**

16. *"When you love and know who you are, you will answer to who God says you are."* **Take a moment to look at how you feel about yourself. Are you happy with who God has created you to be? Are**

you willing to accept that you are not a mistake but a miracle manifested?

17. *"Know your purpose, and when adversity arises, take dominion and authority over it. Press your way into God's plan for your life."* **Have you discovered God's plan for your life? What are they? Are you committed to doing the work to make His plans for your life come to fruition?**

18. *"Even in the midst of the storm God becomes the Calm that settles the wind."* **How do you handle the storms of life?**

"When love is evident faith happens." (Galatians 5:6) *For in Christ Jesus neither circumcision nor uncircumcision avails anything, but faith working through love.*

Conclusion

My prayer is that this book has been a blessing, as well as, an eye opener for women that desire to please God. I wrote God-wife as an inspiration to women everywhere. God has created each of us to live a full and purpose filled life. Marriage is a life-long investment that reaps great returns. As you continue on this journey that we call life, remember that Holy Spirit is our Guide. God honors marriage and the fact that He created marriage for procreation, we are to be examples of what a true God-marriage should be for many generations to come. We can apply the day to day experiences and learn from them. Life will not be a bed of roses, however, faith and fellowship with the Father will always outweigh whatever obstacles come your way.

We are saved by hope and the knowledge of Jesus. He is the glue that holds mankind together. When we trust totally on Him there is nothing that will be impossible to those who believe. Jesus is our inspiration and direction. When we are inspired, we are motivated to follow through with what God has for us in our lives. It is so important that you know that you have what it takes to be a God-wife. It is the next level of the "Good" wife. Why choose to be ordinary when you can live the life of extraordinary.

I trust that every chapter has touched on that very thing you need to take being a wife to newer heights and you begin to see the fruits of your labor! *"In all your ways acknowledge Him, and He shall direct your paths" (Proverbs 3:6 NKJV). Know that today is a new day and the best day to start your journey as a God-wife. When you acknowledge Him, the blessings are yours. Now, walk in them and know that God is faithful and full of wisdom and all understanding.*

Notes

One

The Importance of Setting the Tone of Your Home

- Daily issues of life: We can't let the issues of life affect the way we treat or respond to our spouse
- Gave godly examples of my paternal grandmother and mother
- Giving one another one hundred percent to the marriage
- Being a warrior protecting and defending our family with the Word

Two

Equally Yoked
2 Corinthians 6:14

- Choosing a mate
- Demonstrating your Christian walk
- Being comparable
- Genesis 2:19-24
- Adam & Eve the first example of Best Friends
- Eve being deceived by the enemy
- Imagine God picking the perfect mate, chose the perfect home, and providing everything we could possibly need to survive
- Understanding the power of unity and walking on one accord
- Satan hates authority
- Obedience & paying the price for disobedience

Three

Investing In Intimacy

- Just as we expect intimacy, God expects intimate time with us
- Delighting in the Lord

- Discuss the ministry of Covenant Keeper's Ministry
- The importance of Marriage Ministry
- Words are powerful
- Confession
- Examples of activities that couples can do to enhance their relationship
- Attacks of the enemy
- Intimacy is not just for the bedroom
- Displays of affection
- Being a wife means many self-less moments
- Keeping the flame burning

Four

Forgiveness First
Colossians 3:13 (AMP)

- Infidelity
- Soul ties
- Prayer of Confession
- Protect what God has blessed you with
- Recognizing the anointing on your marriage and husband
- The weapon of prayer
- Dealing with your true hurt feelings

- Forgiving and forgetting; dealing with forgiveness and bitterness

Five

The Other "S" Word

- Submission: the most misunderstood word
- The greatest example of submission
- Walking as a united front
- Submitting to God first
- Submitting to the leadership of your husband

Six

Communication: The Key that Opens the Door

- Men and women interpret information differently
- Communication skills
- Expressing your feelings
- Recognizing your attitude toward your husband
- Passive vs aggressive
- Silence, not the "silent treatment" is golden
- Body language
- There is a way to do everything

- The God-wife knows and understands that her example becomes effortless when she is led by Holy Spirit

Seven

The Inner Circle: Choosing Your Friends Wisely

- True friends are hard to come by
- Biblical healthy friend relationships
- Ruth & Naomi
- Having a lot of friends does not mean that you have healthy relationships
- Be careful of "that girlfriend" that is always willing to give you relationship advice
- Jesus and His inner circle
- Forming a 21 day habit with your husband concerning your time together
- The example of Esther and Jezebel
- Jealousy
- The uniqueness of you

Eight

Know Your Identity: You are Who God says You Are

- We are made special in the sight of God

- Encountering different types of people
- Utilizing the gifts that God gave each of us
- Losing your identity
- See yourself as God sees you
- Labeling: the new trend of today
- Called by name
- Mental, verbal and physical abuse
- You are not a mistake

Nine

The Dynamics of a God-Wife

God first above all else, Virtue always, Values forever

- Setting the standard
- The value of the God-wife
- Creating your list
- The counterfeit
- Household roles
- A wife of many hats
- Pulling double-duty
- A God-wife spends her time wisely
- There is always someone watching
- Wielding the sword of faith
- Handling sudden life hiccups

Ten
Nothing is Too Hot for God

- Definition of fire
- The fire seems too hot to bear
- Isaiah 43:15-19
- A fire guard
- Allowing God to completely absorb that which is trying to devour you
- God's divine purpose
- Nothing is impossible for God

Eleven

Note to the Single Ladies:
Walk in Your Divine Wholeness

- There is a spiritual war going on
- Having a complete relationship with Christ
- Fighting Temptations
- The revelation
- God already has a plan
- Loving yourself enough to respect yourself
- Settling is never an option
- Forsaking Mr. Right for Mr. Right Now
- Making that commitment that you can build upon

- God of a second chance
- Guard your heart
- Evaluating your thought process
- Virtue is a part of your faith

Twelve

The Journey of the God-Wife: Living the Good Life

- The promise is already spoken over your life
- God is preparing you for your season
- Remember the prayer of the righteous avails much power
- Be a reflection of what He sees
- Change your mind-set to the mind of Christ

About the Author

April Young is a native of Hampton Virginia. She is the oldest of six siblings. She is happily married to the love of her life Micheal Young. She is the mother of two adult children Jare'l and Lauren. She is the proud grandmother of two, Jailen and Skye. April was a Christian educator for fifteen years, where she was nominated as Teacher of the Year in 1996 and Employee of the Year in 1998. She was also the owner and operator of All About You Tutoring. She is an active member of Chosen For Completion Ministries (C4C). She and her husband are very active in the community. April enjoys reading and writing short stories, plays, skits, and screenplays. She is the author of several plays and skits. In her spare time she enjoys acting and directing. She also wrote, directed and performed in her first screenplay. April has had the privilege of being a conference speaker, as well as, a mentor to many women. In 2001 and 2002 she received Ministry Leader of the Year awards. She shares the love of cooking and entertaining family and friends with her husband, Micheal. April believes that the Word of God is the ultimate foundation for daily living. Her life changing experiences have been a testimony that has blessed and encouraged many. She is currently working on her next project, a fictional book series. April and her husband Micheal divide their time between South Carolina and Virginia.

Contact the Author

For speaking engagements and conferences you may contact April at:

asygodwife@yahoo.com

CPSIA information can be obtained
at www.ICGtesting.com
Printed in the USA
LVOW11s1742270218
568056LV00002B/391/P